Gombe Stream National Park in Tanzania, 1965.

*Goodall took notes on a pair of chimps she observed in Tanzania in 1987.*

# CONTENTS

# Jane Goodall's Message of Hope Lives On

The British conservationist, who died at age 91, leaves behind a legacy of wisdom, compassion, and optimism for the future.

**BY JEFFREY KLUGER**

THERE ARE FEW PEOPLE IN HUMAN history whose last names alone are sufficient to conjure up kindness, goodness, wisdom, and grace: Mandela, Gandhi, King, Lincoln. Add to that list Goodall. The other four left us years ago. Jane Goodall—zoologist, primatologist, anthropologist, conservationist, winner of the U.S. Presidential Medal of Freedom, and Dame Commander of the Order of the British Empire (DBE)—joined them on October 1, 2025; she died at age 91.

"Dr. Jane Goodall DBE, U.N. Messenger for Peace and founder of the Jane Goodall Institute, has passed away, due to natural causes. She was in California as part of her speaking tour in the United States" the Jane Goodall Institute posted on Instagram. "Dr. Goodall's discoveries as an ethologist revolutionized science, and she was a tireless advocate for the protection and restoration of our natural world."

The spare prose of the announcement was a fitting reflection of the quiet, austere, deliberate way Goodall lived her remarkable life—qualities essential for work that required hours, months, and years crouched in the jungles and clearings of Africa, most notably in the Gombe National Park in Tanzania, observing chimpanzees from a sort of intimate distance and discovering their sometimes loving, sometimes violent, sometimes ingenious lives.

In 1960, Goodall first arrived in Gombe, part of a group of three young naturalists—along with Dian Fossey and Birutė Galdikas—whom famed anthropologist Louis Leakey dispatched to study primates in their natural environment. Leakey playfully dubbed them the Trimates. All three women distinguished themselves. Galdikas has spent more than 50 years studying the orangutans of Indonesian Borneo in their native habitat. Fossey dedicated herself to studying mountain gorillas in their Congo homeland and lost her life in their cause: In 1985 she was murdered in her cabin in Rwanda while working to protect the gorillas from poachers. Goodall had the gift of years—and the gift of patience—and over the decades her discoveries spilled forth.

In 1960, she witnessed a group of chimpanzees eating a bushpig, doing away with the previous belief that chimps were strictly vegetarians.That same year, she made the startling observation that chimps strip the bark from twigs and use the denuded stick to fish for termites in termite mounds—overturning the even more closely held belief that humans are the only animals to use tools.

Chimps, she discovered, mirror humans in other, decidedly less benign ways. From 1974 to 1978, she observed what she dubbed "the Four Year War," an extended, bloody conflict between two groups of rival chimpanzees in Gombe, which she called the main Kasakela group and the Kahama splinter group. During that time, she also observed cannibalism among chimpanzees when a mother and daughter pair stole, killed, and ate babies in their own community, likely to eliminate a line of rival females.

But Goodall discovered a gentle side to chimpanzees, too. They play, they tickle, they kiss, they grieve. They make submissive, gestural apologies after a quarrel. And, in powerful moments of cross-species care, they sometimes accepted her—the quiet, comparatively hairless, human observer—as part of their band.

In 2009, Goodall spoke to TIME's Andrea Sachs about her time in the field and shared some of her most treasured exchanges with the chimps. In one such moment, she was following a young male through the jungle, fighting her way through the brush and the scrub and catching thorns in her hair as the chimp hurried ahead. Finally she reached a clearing, an open space across which the chimp could have easily hurried if he was trying to leave his pur-

*Goodall studied chimps in their natural environment in Gombe Stream National Park in Tanzania. She made handprints with children in Hong Kong in 2016 (opposite).*

suer behind. Instead, she found him sitting quietly, apparently waiting for her. Touched by the gesture, she found a palm nut on the ground—something chimps love—picked it up, and held it out to him. At that moment, however, the chimp wasn't hungry.

"He turned his face away," she recalled. "So I put my hand closer. And he turned, he looked directly in my eyes, he reached out, he took the nut . . . he dropped it, but he very gently squeezed my hand, which is how chimpanzees reassure each other. That was a communication that, for us, predates words."

On another occasion, she was observing a young mother she named Flo and her five-month-old baby, who was just learning to walk. "[Flo] trusts me so much that when he totters towards me and reaches out, she doesn't snatch him away like she used to, but she just keeps her hand protectively around him and she lets him reach out to touch my nose. And this was just so magic."

Flo wasn't alone in trusting Goodall. The billions of members of Goodall's own species did, too. We trusted her to be something of an ambassador between the human nation and that of our closest genetic kin. We trusted her to be an advocate for nature and for conserving the wild world. And it was a trust that was rewarded.

In her final article for TIME (see page 92), in 2021, Goodall took up the cause not of fauna, but of flora, writing about the devastating consequences the planet could suffer as millions of acres of trees are cut, razed, and burned every year. At one time, she wrote, the planet was home to 6 trillion trees. Now that number has been halved, mostly in the last 100 years. She called on readers to support the Trillion Trees campaign, a drive to plant 1 trillion trees by 2030. And she lent her name to a similar effort: the Trees for Jane initiative. From space, Goodall wrote, our planet is a palette of white and blue and brown and green—and the green is in retreat.

"One trillion trees planted and protected is a big number, even over a 10-year period," she wrote. "But if everyone pitches in, we have a fighting chance to make a difference. Together, let's create a sustainable planet for generations to come. Join us today. Let's give our planet a new reason for hope."

In her near century of life, Goodall was all about the hope. In her final conversation with TIME, also in 2021, she said, "I'm about to leave the world with all the mess, whereas young people have to grow up into it. If they succumb to the doom and gloom, that's the end. If you don't hope you sink into apathy; hope is a crucial way to get through this."

Goodall's long, heartening campaign has ended. Let's now see if we're all worthy of her work. ☐

# *a* LIFE *in* PHOTOS

Jane Goodall spent six decades in the public eye. Here, some of her most indelible moments caught on film.

BY SHARON COTLIAR

*When a 26-year-old Jane Goodall and her mother, Vanne, an author, arrived in Tanzania in 1960 and set up a tent to live in, locals "thought we were completely crazy," she recalled to* People *in 2010. "None of them thought I would last more than a couple weeks." Last, she did. A lone Goodall can be seen here typing up her field notes by lamplight.*

*Goodall has a son, Hugo, nicknamed Grub, with first husband Hugo van Lawick, a National Geographic photographer (above, in 1971). "He enabled me to provide proof of things I was describing," she said. The primatologist sometimes hid bananas under her shirt as she approached chimps like Fifi (opposite, in 1964), who grew to accept her after other chimps did.*

"They let me walk up to them, but if somebody else appeared, they'd run away," said Goodall (with Flint, the first wild chimp she studied from infancy, circa 1965).

*"I hope to leave my mark by empowering young people to take action," said Goodall of her more than 150,000-member youth-focused Roots & Shoots program—part of the Jane Goodall Institute—which "began on my porch with just a few students in Dar es Salaam, Tanzania, in 1991. They are creating a better world for generations to come." Here, Goodall celebrated U.N. International Day of Peace in 2003 with Roots & Shoots at her childhood home in Bournemouth, England.*

*While Goodall's research focus was chimpanzees, she championed protections for all primates—including orangutans, like this one she painted with at the Perth Zoo in Australia in 2008. "We celebrate these incredible, intelligent beings and raise awareness about the urgent need to protect them," she wrote on Facebook in 2024. "Orangutans are facing unprecedented threats from habitat loss, deforestation, and illegal wildlife trade."*

*Goodall (left, at a Roots & Shoots event in Austria) left Africa in 1986 and began speaking around the world because, she said, "I had to leave what I loved in order to do what I could to save what I loved." Among her many famous supporters was activist Greta Thunberg (above, in 2020), whom Goodall credited with making a "big impact" on climate change.*

*Using more than 100 hours of forgotten footage captured by Goodall's first husband, van Lawick, director Brett Morgen wove a compelling narrative of the scientist's early work in the 2017 documentary simply titled* Jane. *"When I finally saw the film, it took me right back," Goodall told* Rolling Stone *in 2017.*

OF HECK
ORE BY PHILIP GLASS
DOGWOOF

*In January 2025, Goodall's scientific breakthroughs and global activism were honored with the Presidential Medal of Freedom, presented to her by President Joe Biden. "This recognition reflects the hope and action of so many people who inspire and motivate me every day in the firm belief that together we can and we must save the natural world for ourselves and future generations," Goodall said in a statement.*

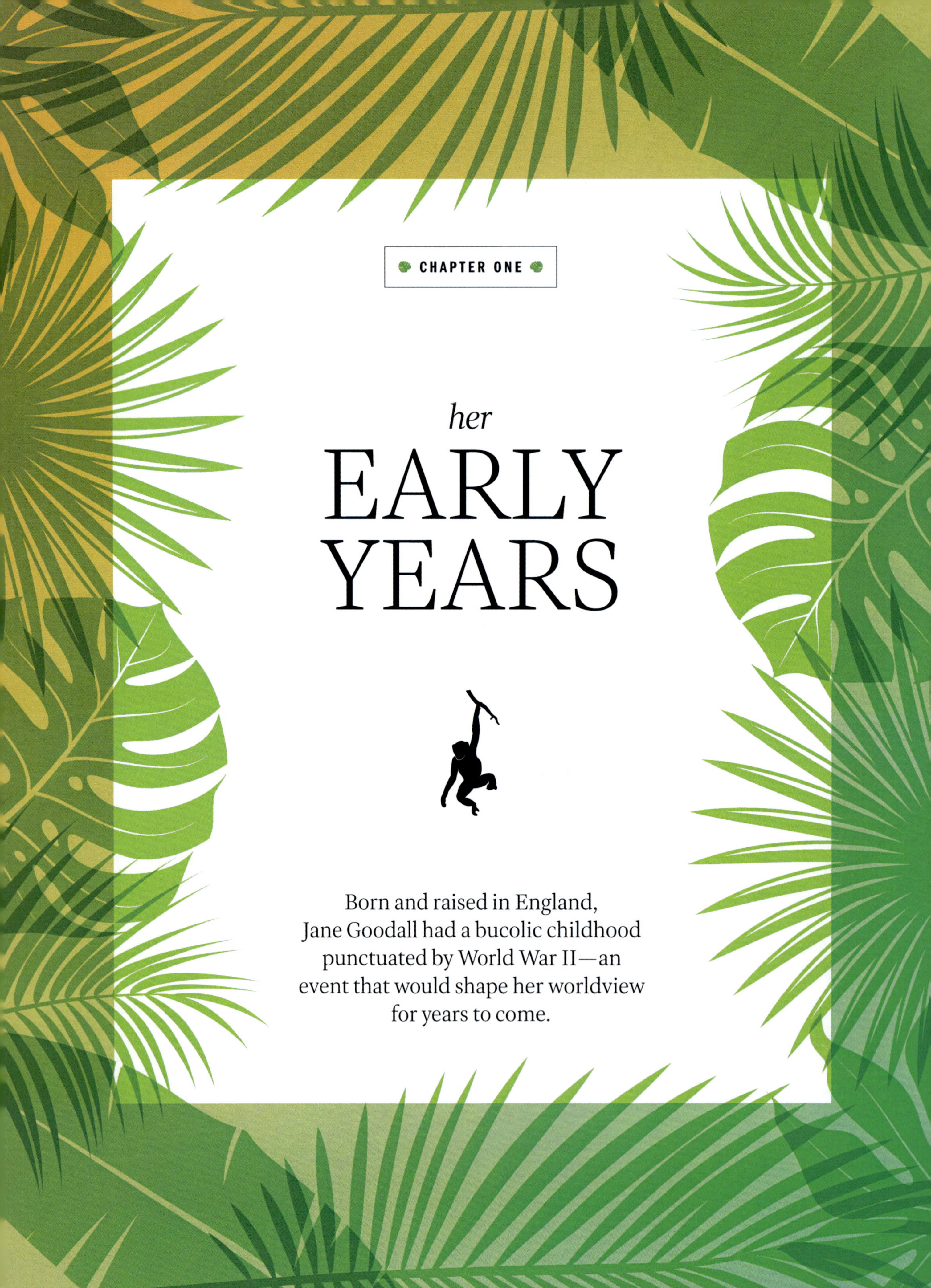

CHAPTER ONE

# *her* EARLY YEARS

Born and raised in England, Jane Goodall had a bucolic childhood punctuated by World War II—an event that would shape her worldview for years to come.

*Chimps were a near-constant presence in Goodall's life from the very beginning. When she was a tot, her father gifted her this stuffed ape named Jubilee.*

# The Making of a Scientist

Goodall's fascination with animals began from a young age—fostered by the nature around her and works of literature like Tarzan and Doctor Dolittle.

**BY RICH SANDS**

THERE WAS NEVER A TIME IN JANE Goodall's childhood when living creatures—including earthworms, dogs, birds, and, of course, chimps—were not the center of her universe. It was a devotion she picked up early and one that would last her entire life. "The holiday I remember most was when I was four and stayed on a farm," she told the U.K.'s *Sunday Times* in 2004. "There, I met pigs, cows, and horses for the first time and helped collect eggs and spread muck. That was probably one of the first moments I realized that I wanted to work with animals."

Born Valerie Jane Morris-Goodall in London on April 3, 1934, a young Goodall once hid away in a barn for hours in hopes of seeing a chicken lay an egg, leading her family to call the police because they believed she'd gone missing. This fascination was further cultivated by the Doctor Dolittle novels of Hugh Lofting, whose title character could communicate with animals, and the Tarzan books by Edgar Rice Burroughs, which she would enjoy in an atypical way: "Like most children before the age of TV and computer games, I loved being outside," she said in the 2017 National Geographic documentary *Jane*. "Playing in the secret places in the garden, learning about nature. I spent many hours high above the ground at the top of my favorite tree and I would read up there, in my own leafy and private world."

Goodall would later gleefully admit that she had been jealous of her "wimpy" (fictional) namesake, Jane Porter, who became Tarzan's love interest, but the tales of the young boy raised by apes were an immediate inspiration. "This is when my dream began," she said in the 2010 documentary *Jane's Journey*. "I would grow up, I would go to Africa, I would live with animals, I would write books about them."

This, it would turn out, was not some fleeting childhood wish, but a belief Goodall held strong as she grew up. "I can remember all my life, actually, her saying, 'When I grow up I'm going to go to Africa and watch animals,'" her younger sister, Judy Waters, noted in that same documentary. "And that was just sort of an accepted fact. I don't think we ever really discussed it in depth as children, but it was just what she was going to do."

Of course, in the 1940s, this was considered a rather far-fetched goal. On a practical level, travel to Africa was costly and Goodall's family was not wealthy. She couldn't afford to go to university for the education needed, and even if she could, women were not offered opportunities in scientific field research at the time. "When I was a little girl, I used to dream as a man, because I wanted to do things that women didn't do back then such as traveling to Africa, living with wild animals, and writing books," she wrote in a 2018 essay for TIME. "I didn't have any female explorers or scientists to look up to, but I was inspired by Doctor Dolittle, Tarzan, and Mowgli in *The Jungle Book*—all male characters."

Though most people laughed off her dreams, her mother provided encouragement. "I think the most important part about my mother was that she listened," Goodall said in *Jane*. Margaret Myfanwe Joseph, a novelist who used the pen name Vanne Morris-Goodall, nurtured her daughter's ambitions. "She was always fair. She was never angry without a reason. She supported me and my love of animals," Goodall remembered. "She never said, 'Well, you're just a girl, you can't do that. Why don't you dream about something you can achieve?' Which is what everybody else told me. So it was my mother who really built up my self-esteem."

Goodall didn't have much of a relationship with her father. Mortimer Herbert Morris-Goodall was a telephone cable testing engineer and also a race car driver for Aston Martin. He went off to fight in World War II when Goodall was five years old, and that was essentially the last time that he was in her life much. "Of course I hugely admired him, but he didn't really care about children," she said.

During the war, Goodall was frequently woken in the middle of the night by sirens warning of air raids by German bombers. The wartime experience had a profound impact on her worldview. "I'm actually glad I grew up in those war years, because I learned to take nothing for granted," she said in a 2020 episode of the *Jane Goodall Hopecast* podcast. "Food was rationed, clothes were rationed. Petrol was rationed. Everything was rationed. And we got, I think it was one square of chocolate a week. We valued every single thing that we had."

After the war, her father's sister married a British government official and was living in Germany, which provided an unlikely opportunity. "Of course we hated the Nazis and thought everything to do with Germany was horrible and evil," Jane told the *New York Times* in 2019. "So Mom sent me off to live with a German family because she wanted me to understand Germans weren't evil, it was the regime."

Mortimer Morris-Goodall stayed in the military, and a few years later, Goodall's parents divorced. One legacy of her father, however, was his gift of a stuffed chimpanzee doll that she named Jubilee. She would hold on to that plaything throughout her life, and as an adult she would bring a similar one, a monkey named Mr. H, with her on her extensive global touring in the name of conservation.

Following her parents' split, Goodall lived with her mother, sister, grandmother, and two aunts in Bournemouth, along England's south coast. She remained enchanted by wildlife, and in 1946, at the age of 12, she started the Alligator Society, a club devoted to observing and reading about animals. The requirements for membership were straightforward: "You have to be able to recognize 10 birds, 10 dogs, 10 trees, and five butterflies OR moths."

Goodall would explore the countryside and watch animals as her passion grew. She attended the Uplands School in nearby Poole and then, with an eye toward saving money for a trip abroad, worked as a secretary and then as a waitress.

She rejected the traditional paths presented to women in that era but humored an uncle who arranged for her to be presented as a debutante for "a kind of marriage market" at court. "[S]o I lined up in Buckingham Palace to shake hands with the Queen," she wrote for TIME. "I remember being surrounded by girls who said to me, 'Don't you dream of being a lady-in-waiting?' I replied, 'Absolutely not—I want to live among wild animals.' They recoiled in horror. They thought

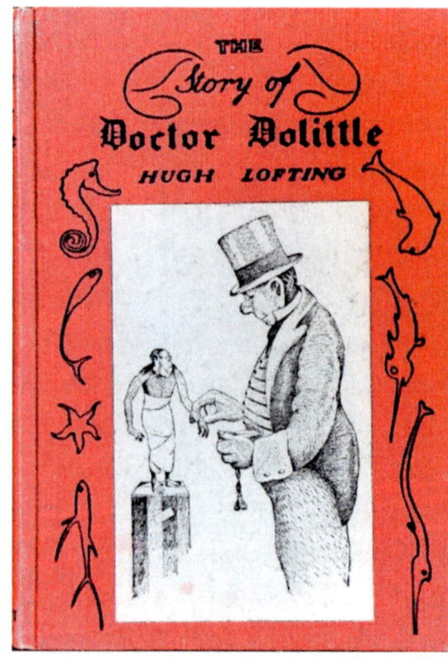

*Goodall in 1954 with her beloved dog Rusty. As a child, she was inspired by the works of Hugh Lofting and Edgar Rice Burroughs (opposite).*

*Paleoanthropologist Louis Leakey, examining what was believed to be a skull from one of the earliest humans, became a mentor to Goodall.*

I was very weird, but then I thought they were very weird, too."

In 1957, she finally was presented with the opportunity she'd long hoped for: A school friend who had moved with her family to a farm outside Nairobi, Kenya, invited Goodall to visit, and she paid for her boat fare with the wages she'd saved. She arrived in Nairobi on her twenty-third birthday, and before seeking a local job, she briefly enjoyed an idyllic life. "We walked in the forest, rode horses, went to parties, and had boyfriends," she later told the *Sunday Times*. She also made frequent trips to the Coryndon Museum in Nairobi, where paleoanthropologist Louis Leakey was working as the curator. Born in Kenya to British missionary parents, he was studying the origins of the human race, convinced that the evolutionary trail of Homo sapiens began in Africa millions of years ago.

Showing the gumption that would become her trademark, Goodall reached out to Leakey in the hopes of working for him. "We met in his large, untidy office, strewn with piles of papers, fossil bones and teeth, stone tools, and all sorts of other things," she wrote in her 1999 memoir, *Reason For Hope: A Spiritual Journey*. "Louis then took me around the museum and asked me question after question about the various exhibits; fortunately, because I had read so much about Africa and animals, I was able to answer most of them. I think he was impressed that someone with no degree understood words like ichthyology and herpetology."

"I wanted to come as close to talking to animals as I could—to be like Doctor Dolittle."

—JANE GOODALL

He hired her as his secretary and soon invited her on a three-month expedition at the Olduvai Gorge, an area rich in early hominid fossils in the Serengeti plains of northern Tanzania on the border of Kenya. "It was fascinating work, but I still wanted to study living creatures," Goodall told *People* in 1990. "I wanted to come as close to talking to animals as I could—to be like Doctor Dolittle."

Before the trip ended, she got closer to her wish, unexpectedly, on an evening stroll with another assistant. "I sensed something behind me—and looking round saw, about 300 yards away, a young male lion, probably around two years old, full grown, but with his mane just sprouting from his shoulders," Goodall recalled. "He was standing and staring at us. He had almost certainly never seen white women, and he was curious. I had no sense of fear—just excitement."

When Leakey was pursuing funding to commission a field study of the chimpanzee population in the Gombe Stream area off Lake Tanganyika (in what was then a British-administered territory but today is the nation of Tanzania), he knew Goodall was the ideal candidate, her interest, patience, and fearlessness far outweighing her lack of formal scientific education. "He wanted an unbiased mind," she noted in *Jane's Journey*, "and he felt that somebody like that, learning about the chimpanzees and how they live out in the natural environment, would help him to better understand the probable behavior of the Stone Age men and women whose remains he'd been searching for all his life." (Goodall confessed that chimps would not have been her first choice. "I was in love with elephants," she told *People* in 2017. "It was just that [Leakey] offered me chimps, which fit into what I see as the mission of my life.")

Goodall briefly returned to England to learn as much as possible about the primates, including observing animals in zoos. She returned to Africa once Leakey had secured financing, but there was one last hurdle to navigate. "At that time, Tanganyika was a British protectorate, and the government authorities were horrified at the thought of a young white woman going off into the bush," she wrote in *Reason For Hope*. "Louis, however, simply refused to take no for an answer, and eventually they gave in. However, they were adamant on one score—I had to take a European companion. Who should it be? It must be someone with whom I was relaxed, someone who would not compete and would leave me to do the study as I thought best. Who better than my mother? I was overjoyed when she agreed."

In July 1960, 26-year-old Goodall (with her mother and an attendant and cook, Dominic Charles Bandora) made her way into the wild for an adventure that would propel her to household-name status. "I'll never forget when Mum and I arrived at last in our little boat on the Gombe shore," Goodall told *People*. "It was a dry, beautiful day. The hills were lush with green, and after we set up our tents with the help of two African game scouts, I slipped away and climbed up into the hills. I met a troop of barking baboons and knew then that my dream had come true." □

# Meet the Trimates

Anthropologist Louis Leakey hand-selected three women, Goodall included, to research the great apes in the wild.

**BY DANIEL S. LEVY**

**Louis S.B. Leakey** had been working at Tanzania's Olduvai Gorge since the 1930s, scanning and excavating the landscape in his search of skeletal and other remains of humanity's African roots. He became convinced that he needed to better understand our closest living relatives, the great apes, in order to unlock information about our elusive, primal past.

To study these majestic creatures, Leakey assigned three researchers to head out into the field. In 1960, Jane Goodall went to study chimpanzees. In 1967, Dian Fossey arrived in Rwanda to learn more about gorillas. And in 1971, Biruté Galdikas headed to the Southeast Asian island of Borneo to observe orangutans. Leakey dubbed these three women primatologists the Trimates.

Leakey helped secure funding for them from such groups as the National Geographic Society and the Wilkie Foundation. He chose Goodall, Fossey, and Galdikas not only because of their passion—he confided to Galdikas that he believed women were superior researchers. "Women were more perceptive, he claimed, and better able to see details that at the time might seem unimportant," Galdikas noted in her 1995 *Reflections of Eden: My Years with the Orangutans of Borneo*. "Women were also more patient. Finally, he claimed, women did not excite aggressive tendencies in male primates the way men did, however unintentionally."

## Dian Fossey

Born and raised in San Francisco, Fossey was an animal lover from the start and took up horseback riding at the age of six. By college, she was an accomplished equestrian. She began her career in occupational therapy and worked with animals on a farm, but she always wanted to visit Africa. In 1963, she spent all her money and took out a bank loan to do so, meeting Leakey in the process. Three years later, a 34-year-old Fossey officially took her post in Africa, first working in the Congo but having to flee because of political turmoil. She then set up her Karisoke Research Center in Volcanoes National Park in 1967, just across the border in Rwanda. Fossey spent each day in the wild, and the gorillas slowly became accustomed to her. While out in the forest, she took a shine to a young gorilla she named Digit because he had an injured finger, probably from a poacher's trap. National Geographic's 1975 program *Search for the Great Apes* showed Digit looking at Fossey's pencil and notebook. Fossey comments, "Sometimes it was hard to tell who was the observer and who was the observed."

In 1970, Fossey enrolled in a doctoral program at Cambridge and completed her degree in 1974. When she returned to Rwanda as a full-fledged scientist, she had been transformed into a fierce activist. "She started doing what she called

*The so-called Trimates comprise Dian Fossey (above, left), who studied gorillas in Rwanda; Biruté Galdikas (above, right), who studies orangutans in Borneo; and Goodall (opposite, with Leakey).*

active conservation," Dr. Tara Stoinski, president, CEO, and chief scientific officer of the Dian Fossey Gorilla Fund, told LIFE. "She hired trappers to go into the field to remove snares. She threatened locals she felt were endangering gorillas, tagged cattle with spray paint so she could identify livestock, and told farmers not to bring them into the forest." Fossey similarly sparred with bushmeat poachers and those looking for trophies like ape hands to make into ashtrays.

In 1977, poachers attacked Digit and his family. While Digit fought them off, his pregnant mate, Simba, and other members escaped. After the poachers killed Digit, they hacked off his hands and head. Fossey had his body brought to her camp to be buried. Digit's death made national news, and Fossey set up a fund to raise money for the protection of gorillas. Her in-your-face activism is likely to have been the cause of her murder, in her cabin in Rwanda in 1985.

Fossey is buried beside Digit, and her death and the 1988 film *Gorillas in the Mist* (starring Sigourney Weaver) focused attention on her life, her activism, and the plight of gorillas.

## Biruté Galdikas

Galdikas took a similarly assertive approach when she arrived in Borneo, confronting village families keeping orangutans as pets by going into their homes to confiscate the animals. "One of the things that I used to say when I would talk to somebody who had an orangutan [is] 'Only the president of Indonesia has the right to keep an orangutan. Are you the president?' And they would say, 'No,' " Galdikas told LIFE. She then took away the animal.

Galdikas's love of apes started when she was a first-grader in Toronto. The first book that she checked out of the local library was *Curious George*. By the second grade, she was determined to be an explorer. When she was an undergraduate at UCLA, she first heard about a young British woman living with chimpanzees. Then while studying for her master's degree in anthropology, she came across a magazine article on orangutans. "I dreamed of going to the great forests of the Far East to study orangutans. I became obsessed with the idea," she recalled in *Reflections of Eden*. Galdikas started writing letters, seeking work in Borneo. She met Leakey when he spoke at UCLA. He interviewed her the next day and eventually drummed up funding so she could fulfill her dream.

A 25-year-old Galdikas arrived with her then husband, Rod Brindamour, in 1971 in Tanjung Puting Reserve, home to the largest number of Bornean orangutans. While she started to get to know individuals, it took years for them to become habituated to her presence. As she searched for the apes, she rigorously gathered data on their activities, the foods they ate—everything from figs, lychees, and breadfruit to termites, caterpillars, leeches, gibbons, bird eggs, and tree rats—identified their calls, and marveled at the forest.

Galdikas has since established a major complex for orangutans. In 1998, she opened the Orangutan Care Center and Quarantine facility in the nearby village of Pasir Panjang to care for confiscated orangutans and prepare them for reintroduction to the wild. The center houses more than 300 orangutans. Galdikas, now 79, has spent more than half a century studying orangutans. Humans and orangutans, she notes, might have diverged millions of years ago, but they share an ancient historical and biological bond.

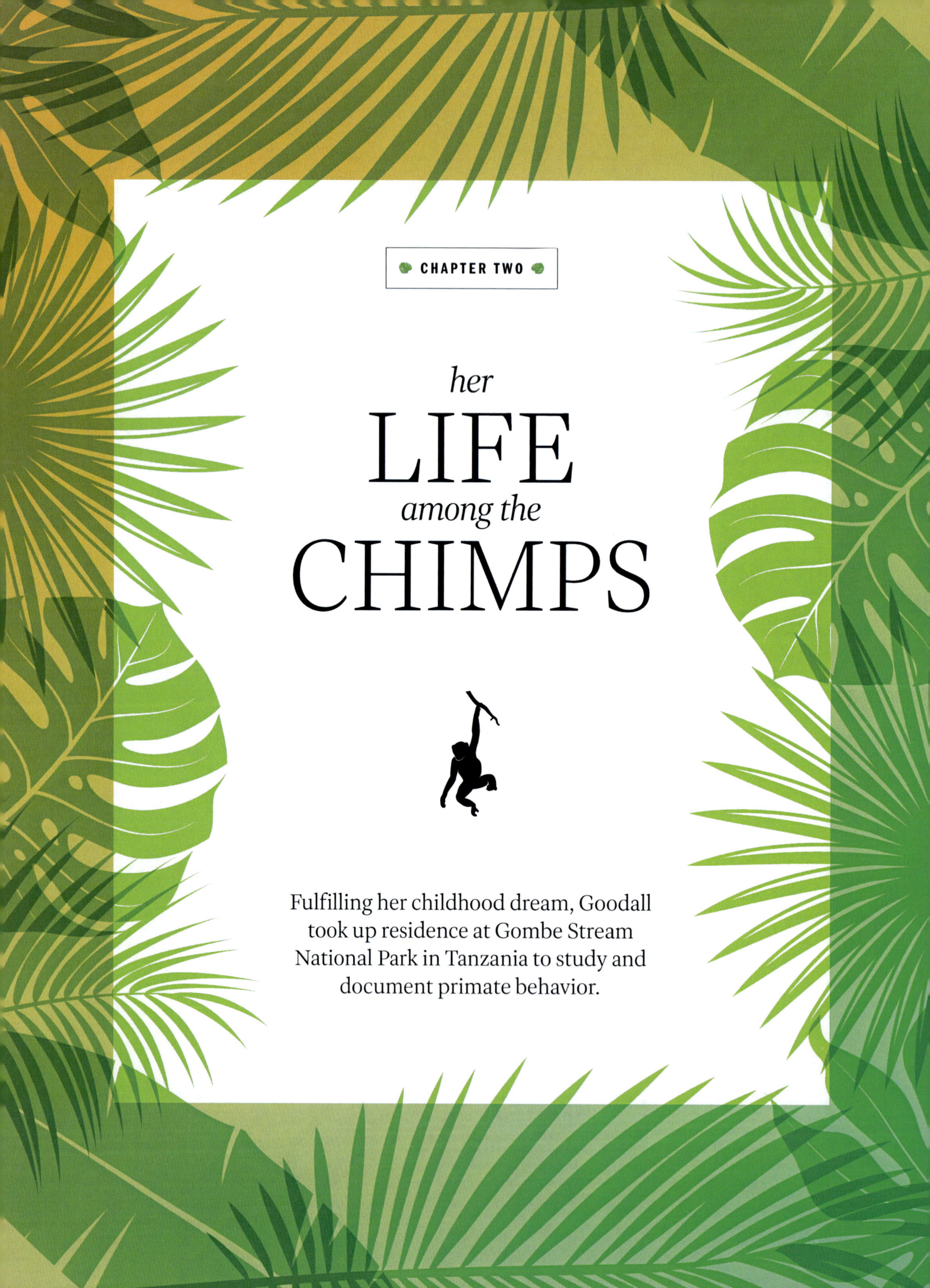

CHAPTER TWO

# *her* LIFE *among the* CHIMPS

Fulfilling her childhood dream, Goodall took up residence at Gombe Stream National Park in Tanzania to study and document primate behavior.

*Goodall, perched in her camp, was visited by a pair of chimps, including one she named Fifi.*

# Uncovering the Human-Ape Connection

Goodall's unconventional approach led to findings that upended much of what scientists believed about chimps.

**BY GINA McINTYRE**

When Jane Goodall stepped off the *Kibisi*, the boat that had delivered her to the Gombe Stream Chimpanzee Reserve on the eastern shore of Lake Tanganyika in what is now Tanzania, on July 14, 1960, she walked into paradise.

"It is so beautiful, with the crystal clear blue lake, the tiny white pebbles on the beach, the sparkling ice cold mountain stream, the palm nut trees, the comical baboons," she wrote in a letter to her family in England excerpted in Dale Peterson's biography *Jane Goodall: The Woman Who Redefined Man*. "Can you wonder that I should be happy here? It is the Africa of my childhood's dreams, and I have the chance of finding out things which no one has ever known before."

The discoveries Goodall would make in Gombe surpassed anything she could have imagined in those early days. Over the next several months, the amateur zoologist uncovered astonishing truths that came to upend the scientific community's fundamental understanding of both humans and primates. Among the most important was her observation that chimpanzees could make and use tools to assist them in their daily lives, something previously believed to be the exclusive province of Homo sapiens and that suggested both species were descended from a common ancestor.

Apart from her findings, Goodall's approach to her work in Gombe was revolutionary in itself, as most studies were then conducted in a laboratory setting rather than in an animal's natural habitat. Her view—that these magnificent creatures were as unique and distinctive as people and just as deserving of consideration and respect—set a new global standard.

"I think it's now generally accepted that we are not the only beings on the planet with personalities, minds and emotions," Goodall told *Vox* in 2021. "That we are part of and not separated from the rest of the animal kingdom."

**Although Goodall would** spend countless hours on her own in the wild, she was never entirely alone in Gombe, particularly at the start of her life-changing excursion, as her mother, Vanne Morris-Goodall, who had long been a source of significant support, accompanied her for most of her expedition. The pair shared a tent, with their meals prepared by a cook they'd brought with them from the city of Kigoma, Dominic Charles Bandora.

Following a confrontation with a group of local fishermen and villagers—who suspected that the Goodalls were there to exaggerate the number of chimpanzees, thereby ensuring Gombe's status as protected territory off-limits to them—several local men were hired as assistants in various roles, one of which was to monitor that Goodall's work was done correctly. But once she set off to undertake her initial exploration of the region and begin her research, she found that her stamina was greater than that of her male field staff members. Addressing their complaints of hunger and exhaustion frequently frustrated Goodall, who could survive on little food and was prepared to work from dawn to dusk, traversing difficult terrain in the search for chimps.

Making compromises for her staff was only one of the setbacks she faced early on in Gombe, however. Roughly one month after her arrival, she and Vanne, who had set up a medical clinic near the camp, both contracted what was probably malaria. Suffering fevers of 104 and 105 degrees and throbbing headaches, mother and daughter could do little more than lie in their tent for days on end. Ultimately, though, even a potentially fatal illness couldn't keep Goodall bedbound; even though she was still experiencing symptoms, she set out again on her mission, determined to observe and record details about the chimps living in the reserve.

"As soon as I began to feel better, I was desperate to continue my work with the chimps," Goodall wrote in *Reason for Hope*. "And so, one morning early, when it was cool, I climbed, slowly and with many pauses, the steep slope opposite our tent. It was a red-letter day, a turning point, for I discovered the Peak, and from that day on, my luck changed. . . . I gradually began to piece together something of the daily life of the Gombe chimpanzees, and my fear of failure began to subside."

Indeed, after overcoming those initial hurdles, her circumstances began to look up. Her initial companions were replaced by expert trackers, who arrived at the beginning of September. They would often split up, allowing Goodall to work quietly and take diligent notes about every aspect of the chimpanzees she saw: their anatomy, their grooming habits, their vocalizations, their movements, their arboreal nesting habits. She began to assign names to the ones she noticed most frequently, not realizing that conventional scientists only referred to their specimens by numbers.

Her diligence was remarkable, and on the morning of October 30, she was rewarded with a landmark discovery: the first recorded eyewitness account of wild chimps consuming the meat of what Goodall would later deduce as an infant bushpig. Previously, chimpanzees were believed to be herbivores, adhering to a diet of fruits, berries, and nuts, much like their fellow great apes. But as Goodall watched through binoculars, she witnessed a bearded male chimpanzee chewing away on a knot of pink flesh while seated in the branch of a tree, a female and her infant attempting to convince him to share his prize.

On November 4, Goodall made an even more surprising discovery. Following a trail above the Linda Valley, she passed a termite mound and noticed a male chimp strip a long stalk of grass of its leaves. He

*"Understanding what chimpanzees are like has made me realize that we humans are not so different from other animals as we used to think," Goodall (here and opposite) would later write in her 1988 book,* My Life With the Chimpanzees.

*Goodall was accompanied to Africa by her mother, Vanne (here, in 1962). Goodall handed out bananas to a waiting chimp in 1964 (opposite).*

plunged the stalk inside the mound, and when he withdrew it, numerous insects were clinging to the grass. He quickly consumed them and then repeated the same set of motions. Two days later, she witnessed the same chimp performing the same ritual at the same termite mound—this time with another male.

Incredibly, Goodall noticed that the bearded male she'd seen eating meat was the same chimp she'd witnessed on both occasions at the termite mound. She dubbed him David Greybeard (see page 48), not realizing at that point that of all the chimps she studied, he would be the one with whom she would form the strongest connection.

Throughout the weeks she'd spent in Gombe, Goodall had made regular reports to her supportive sponsor, Louis Leakey, about her observations, but her discovery that chimps were fashioning tools was so significant that he famously cabled her a weighty reply: "Now we must redefine *tool*, redefine *man*, or accept chimpanzees as humans."

**GOODALL'S INITIAL SOJOURN** to Gombe concluded on December 1, 1960, only weeks after Vanne's November 12 departure, and in the subsequent months, Leakey undertook twin efforts on Goodall's behalf. The first was to help her gain admission to Cambridge so that she might obtain a Ph.D. in ethology, the study of animal behavior—something of a gamble considering that Goodall had no undergraduate degree, having attended only secretarial school.

Yet Leakey felt it was important for Goodall to receive a doctorate, understanding that her findings would be seen as more credible if she had obtained the appropriate credentials. The second was to try to obtain additional backing so that she might have the means to return to Gombe to continue her research. Perhaps unsurprisingly, the charismatic Leakey succeeded on both fronts.

With Leakey having convinced National Geographic's Research and Exploration Committee to fund Goodall's work for several more months, Goodall deferred her Cambridge enrollment until the end of 1961 and spent the bulk of the year working in Gombe, this time without a European chaperone. Bandora returned as camp cook, bringing along his family, as well as two additional staff.

But the bulk of her time was spent as the sole human wandering through the wilds of "Chimpland" as Goodall described the landscape in her letters to her family, and her journeys led to more incredible discoveries. For Goodall, one of the most unforgettable was witnessing a performance that she began to think of as a "rain dance," in which two groups of chimps would leap into trees before hurling themselves down to the ground once more amid the torrents of a thunderstorm.

Enduring extreme weather conditions, sometimes battling insomnia, even developing shingles at one point, Goodall was nevertheless entirely devoted to her work. She was rewarded by regular visits from David Greybeard, who, astonishingly, had begun to venture into the primatologist's camp.

Sometimes, he'd help himself to bananas Goodall provided; on other occasions, he would climb the palm tree to sample ripe palm nuts.

Goodall was delighted to have an opportunity to so closely observe such an intriguing subject, describing him in her letters to home as a "lovely specimen. All his hair, scarcely any baldness of the forehead, long cheek hair, dark handsom face—very handsom chimp." (For all Goodall's gifts, proper spelling was never among them, as she herself was the first to admit.)

After a total of 15 months in Gombe, Goodall began her doctorate program at Cambridge, dividing her time between Africa and England, though she would have preferred to remain focused on the chimps full time. "I was only doing this thesis for Leakey's sake," Goodall told the BBC in March 2014. "I'd never had an ambition to be a scientist and be part of academia." Her misgivings were exacerbated by the reception she received from her male colleagues, who were baffled by her decision to identify the apes by names and take note of their personalities. "Some scientists actually said I must have taught them (to use tools). That would have been fabulous if I could have done that."

When Goodall returned to the field in July of 1962, it was with a commission from *National Geographic* to write a 7,500-word article for the magazine and to photograph the chimps as she was able (previous attempts to capture images of her work had yielded mixed results). The editors had also hired an esteemed wildlife photographer Hugo van Lawick. Born in Indonesia and raised in England and the Netherlands, van Lawick had spent time living in Nairobi, Kenya, where he became acquainted with Louis Leakey through his son, Richard Leakey.

Van Lawick arrived in August, and from the start, Hugo and Jane, two people of similar temperament who shared an abiding passion for the natural world, got along well, even though he smoked and Jane could not abide the habit. But both Goodall and her chimps quickly came to accept his presence.

"The chimpanzees have become so much tamer since last year, and they have accepted the presence of Hugo van Lawick with his tripods and lenses in the most wonderful way," Goodall wrote to Leonard Carmichael, secretary of the Smithsonian Institution and Chairman of the National Geographic Society's Committee for Research and Exploration, in a letter quoted in Peterson's biography. "The method I have always followed—never hiding from the chimpanzees, never following them when they have moved away from me, and never appearing particularly interested in them—has, at long last, paid dividends."

Concerned about the seeming impropriety of Goodall's spending hours alone with a male photographer, the *National Geographic* paid for Vanne to return to Gombe to again serve as chaperone. During his months at the camp, van Lawick photographed the rugged jungle terrain and captured numerous images of chimps perched high in tree branches as well as many, many photos of Goodall herself and the daily rhythms of her life in Gombe: the naturalist seated beside the bold David Greybeard; Jane washing her hair in the Kakombe Stream; Vanne dispensing medicine to local villagers.

*Goodall formed a professional—then personal—relationship with wildlife photographer Hugo van Lawick, whom she married in London in 1964.*

*This still from the 1965 CBS TV special* Miss Goodall and the World of Chimpanzees *has become one of the most enduring images of Goodall in the field.*

When Goodall's first-person account was finally published in the August 1963 issue of the *National Geographic*, it ran for 37 pages, detailing all her revolutionary findings. Illustrated with photos taken by both Jane and Hugo, "My Life Among Wild Chimpanzees" detailed Goodall's goals: "The primary aim of my field study was to discover as much as possible about the way of life of the chimpanzee before it is too late—before encroachments of civilization crowd out, forever, all nonhuman competitors. Second, there is the hope that results of this research may help man in his search toward understanding himself... Knowledge of social traditions and culture of such an animal, studied under natural conditions, could throw new light on the growth and spread of early human cultures."

She went on to describe the trove of discoveries

"The primary aim of my field study was to discover as much as possible about the way of life of the chimpanzee before it is too late."

**—JANE GOODALL**

that she'd made: Chimpanzees are nomadic within their territory, traveling as many as eight or 10 miles per day and typically moving in small groups. At night, each makes his own nest—except for mothers who sleep with infants until about the age of three. The little chimps will often play games together, just as human children do. Goodall also took note of the chimps' habit of mutual grooming as "an important part of the social life of chimpanzees... [with] two friends, or even a small group, [sitting] quietly for hours searching through each other's long black hair for specks of dirt, grass, seeds, or ticks."

Additionally, she wrote about the rain dance ritual she had observed; about the chimps as carnivores consuming the remains of a colobus monkey and an antelope; about their occasional clashes with baboons, the chimps' only serious competitor

*David Greybeard (above) became an important ally for Goodall to break into the chimp community. Goodall's partnership with van Lawick (opposite, middle) allowed the world to not only hear about but see her work.*

for food; and about their use of twigs and long grasses to to extract termites from inside the insects' mounds. She concluded with an acknowledgment that there was "still much to learn about the behavior of the free-ranging chimpanzee," and announced her plans to return to the Gombe Stream Reserve for additional study.

By the time the article appeared—mailed directly to 3 million regular subscribers—Goodall had already gone back to Africa to resume her research, but she quickly began to understand the profound impact that the story would have on her life. Captivating the public imagination, it catapulted her to a level of celebrity and success she might never have imagined, though fame brought with it additional scrutiny, often manifesting as overt sexism.

"The other scientists were scornful at first of the findings of this young girl, and they said I only got credit because *National Geographic* came in with grant money to fund my project because I had nice legs," Goodall recalled to Margaret Atwood during a 2022 conversation for the Australian edition of *Harper's Bazaar*. "If that was said now, it would be shocking. But back then, I thought, 'Well, thank you, legs.'"

**THE YEAR 1963** was a landmark for Goodall in ways beyond the mere publication of the *National Geographic* article. On December 26, when Goodall was back in Bournemouth to celebrate the Christmas holiday with her family, she received a telegram with a proposal reading, "Will you marry me stop Hugo." Jane answered yes, and the couple wed on Easter, March 28, 1964, at London's Chelsea Old Church. According to Peterson's biography, the wedding cake was topped with a clay model of David Greybeard.

When the happy couple returned to Gombe, there was a new addition to the chimpanzee brood. One of the high-ranking females that Goodall had made a habit of observing, Flo, had given birth to a new male infant dubbed Flint. Able to closely follow his development, Goodall took note of the first tentative steps that Flint took and how his mother cradled him when he collapsed as an act of reassurance. As he aged, his older sister, Fifi, spent more time cavorting with him, caring for her younger sibling and allowing Flo to rest.

Flo, Fifi, and Flint were among the chimps who

CONTINUED ON PAGE 50

# The Legacy of David Greybeard

He was the first chimp to connect with Goodall—and he would help provide some of her most profound discoveries.

BY AVA ERICKSON

**In July 1960,** Jane Goodall started observing the chimpanzees in the Gombe Stream National Park in Tanzania. For many months, she watched them from afar with binoculars. By the fall, she had already made some groundbreaking observations, but she had yet to make any close contact with the animals. To gain their trust, Goodall began leaving bananas by her cabin for them to collect.

One day, a chimpanzee with a patch of gray hair on his chin ventured down from the mountains to take a banana, and Goodall followed him back into the forest. At one point, she thought she had lost him, but when she turned a corner, she found him, seemingly waiting for her. She cautiously sat next to him and offered him a red palm nut, a chimp favorite, from her hand. At first, he turned away, but when she extended her hand a little closer, he looked directly into her eyes, took the nut, dropped it, and gently squeezed her fingers, a gesture of reassurance among chimpanzees.

Though he didn't want the nut, this moment marked the beginning of a rare closeness and mutual trust between Goodall and a chimpanzee, whom she named David Greybeard for his distinctive patch of hair. Greybeard would become her favorite and most important companion in the field, playing a pivotal role in her studies as the first chimp that Goodall observed using tools and eating meat, and most important, for their intense bond, which permitted her close observation of the group of chimpanzees in Gombe Stream National Park.

## Tools and Diet

Prior to her first direct contact with David Greybeard, Goodall had observed him and another male chimp using a stick to fish termites out of a termite hill. In her field notebook she wrote, "I could see a little better the use of the piece of straw. It was held in the left hand, poked onto the ground, and then removed coated with termites. The straw was then raised to the mouth and the insects picked off with the lips, along the length of the straw, starting in the middle." This was the first time chimps were observed utilizing tools (she later saw them using leaves for drinking and cleaning, and opening nuts with stones). Previously, it was believed that only humans used tools, so upon reporting her observations to her boss, paleoanthropologist and archaeologist Louis Leakey, he responded, "Now we must redefine *tool*, redefine *man*, or accept chimpanzees as human."

Equally revolutionary was Goodall's discovery that chimps eat meat. It was previously thought that they only ate plants, differentiating them from their human counterparts, but Goodall observed David Greybeard (and later other chimps in her observation group) eating bushpig and colobus monkey, and even hunting.

## Bonding with David Greybeard

Although many of Goodall's key discoveries were first observed in David Greybeard, it was their connection that transformed the study of primatology. Over time, Greybeard began to approach Jane on his own, letting her observe his daily routines and interactions with other chimps.

He had a gentle temperament

*David Greybeard and Goodall in 1965.*

and would frequently bring other chimps to her camp and introduce them to her, which allowed her to further study the group. "The other chimps would see David sitting there, not running away, and so gradually they'd think, 'Well, she can't be so scary, after all.' He had a wonderful, gentle disposition. He was really loved by other chimps; the low-ranking ones would go to him for protection. He wasn't terribly high-ranking, but he had a very high-ranking friend, Goliath. And there was just something about him. He had a very handsome face, his eyes wide apart, and this beautiful gray beard," Goodall told Bill Moyers in 2010.

Goodall's relationship with David revealed the possibility of trust, empathy, and communication between humans and chimpanzees, our closest relatives, shining a new light on the level of intelligence and social complexity these animals are capable of.

David Greybeard is believed to have died during a 1986 pneumonia epidemic, but his legacy lives on. In 2013, he was named one of TIME's 15 most influential animals, and Goodall herself said that she hoped to be greeted by him on the other side.

CONTINUED FROM PAGE 47

appeared with Goodall on the cover of the December 1965 issue of *National Geographic*. The magazine contained the second article by Goodall, "New Discoveries Among Africa's Chimpanzees" (which appeared under her married name, Baroness Jane van Lawick-Goodall, with photography by her husband) and featured a prominent discussion of Flo, whom Goodall described as "ugly," elaborating: "She is so old that her teeth are worn down to the gums. She has a deformed, bulbous nose, a ragged ear with a great piece torn out, and hardly any chin at all. Yet she has as much character as a whole platoon of the other chimps." Commenting on the bonds between Flo and her children, she noted that "chimps are promiscuous, and the father is not a part of the family." Of all of van Lawick's images featured in the story, it was a shot of Goodall, dressed in a loose tan shirt and khaki shorts, hair pulled back into her signature ponytail, touching hands with young Flint as she crouched close to the ground, that generated special attention. "When I saw it, though I did not realize it would become iconic, it did make me think of Michelangelo's painting of God reaching out to Man," Goodall said in a 2023 interview with the BBC.

The impact of the image grew in time. "[It] forced science to abandon the idea that humans were the only sentient beings with personalities, minds, and emotions," Goodall told the BBC. "Thus [this image] opened up a whole new way of understanding who animals are and showed that we humans are a part of and not separated from the rest of the animal kingdom."

Debuting in conjunction with the issue, the one-hour television documentary *Miss Goodall and the Wild Chimpanzees*, narrated by preeminent actor and filmmaker Orson Welles, was broadcast on CBS on December 22, 1965, to an estimated 25 million viewers in North America. The exposure further burnished Goodall's growing reputation as the world's foremost expert in primatology, her achievements helping to begin to knock down outdated sexist prohibitions against women pursuing careers in the sciences. Goodall continued to break boundaries, earning her Ph.D. in ethology in 1966.

As husband and wife lived together in the African wilderness, van Lawick continued to studiously document all of Goodall's interactions with the chimps in still images and on film. He and Jane had both taken issue with certain aspects of the CBS documentary—Goodall was angry that she'd been shown washing her hair; a shot of a leopard was pulled from stock footage; the voiceover narration contained inaccuracies—and the pair hoped to make further films together, exercising more creative control.

While Gombe always remained Goodall's primary focus, she and Hugo traveled to other sites in Africa

*Goodall gave birth to son Hugo Eric Louis van Lawick in 1967. He goes by the affectionate nickname "Grub" to this day. Opposite: Mother and son wrangled a wild dog.*

*Goodall in 1974.*

as well. The couple spent time in the Serengeti, traveling in a specially outfitted VW bus that *National Geographic* had paid to customize, where they happened across a scene of Egyptian vultures using stones to break open ostrich eggs that had been left abandoned in a nest. It inspired an article on tool use among animals that was published in *Nature* under Jane and Hugo's joint byline on December 24, 1966.

The year brought disheartening revelations as well, though, with a polio outbreak tearing through Gombe. Six chimps died or disappeared, and six more were left partially paralyzed. "It was a horrible time," Goodall recalled in the 2017 documentary *Jane*. "One after another, chimpanzees came in, dragging limbs . . . It was awful." Leaping into action, Goodall and Hugo acquired medication to stop the spread of the disease, inserting doses of the treatment into bananas, then keeping meticulous records to ensure that the chimps visiting the feeding areas that

"I see no difference between helping a human and helping an animal."

—JANE GOODALL

had been established received the correct amount.

The actions came too late to save Mr. McGregor, one of the chimps Goodall had observed for the longest time. The chimp, who had lost function in multiple limbs, had to be shot. "I couldn't watch an animal suffering, any more than I could watch a human suffering and not help if I could," Goodall said in *Jane*. "I see no difference between helping a human and helping an animal. I mean, yes, we could have gone on and fed him every day and kept him alive for what reason? To be honest, if that happens to me, I do not wish to be kept alive either."

While expanding their footprint of scientific inquiry, Hugo and Jane also expanded their family, welcoming a son, Hugo Eric Louis van Lawick, on March 4, 1967. Although the demands of caring for the newborn, nicknamed "Grub," prevented Goodall from spending the entirety of her days in the field, she quickly found that the experience of becoming

CONTINUED ON PAGE 56

*Baboons, not chimps, flanked Goodall and van Lawick on an outing in 1974.*

CONTINUED FROM PAGE 53

a mother helped her gain a greater understanding of the behaviors of mother chimps.

"I understood, for example, when a chimpanzee mother is approached by another one, and she gets all angry if the child is asleep or something, I've felt exactly the same—these surges of irrational anger if something happens that you think is going to harm or disturb your own child," she told interviewer Steve Paulson in 2017. "So, I could much better understand the mother chimpanzees when they behaved in what seemed to be the same way.

"I really looked on Flo [the chimp] as a role model as well," Goodall continued. "She was patient and supportive. She was protective but not overprotective. She could impose discipline when she wanted. She provided a nice secure base for her kids. And she supported them if they got into difficulties. That's the hallmark of a good human mother."

Although Goodall had spent most of the first few months of Grub's life at the family home in Limuru, Kenya, she returned to Gombe with the baby by midsummer, working and writing while caring for Grub. A protective enclosure was built for the boy, designed to keep him safe from any chimps that might be out hunting for food. "But you could stand upright and walk across [the enclosure]," Goodall told Fox News in 2018. "He couldn't even crawl. So, it was almost like a giant cot. And he was never on his own."

*Years in Africa allowed Goodall and her family to take in all manner of wildlife—including lions (above) and more baboons (opposite).*

Grub would travel with his parents across Africa—Hugo's commission with *National Geographic* ended in 1968, and he was keen to embark on a passion project about East African carnivores that took him to the Serengeti, nearly 500 miles from Gombe. With its herds of wildebeests and zebras and prides of lions, the region was endlessly fascinating to van Lawick in the same way Gombe and its chimps were to Goodall.

Although she traveled with Hugo and Grub, Jane remained committed to her own work. The reserve was now officially Tanzania's Gombe National Park, and her camp had become a respected institution known as the Gombe Stream Research Center, which hosted students and other researchers from around the world. As the next several years passed, the couple spent less and less time together, eventually drifting apart. They divorced in 1974, though they remained on good terms, co-parenting Grub and collaborating on various projects.

"He wanted me to leave Gombe because there was no way he could stay and work, but I couldn't," Goodall says in *Jane*. "It was my life, and he had his."

**ONCE GRUB WAS** old enough to attend school, Goodall brought him to England to live with her

*Goodall married her second husband, Derek Bryceson, in 1975.*

mother, Vanne, in Bournemouth; she would visit at Christmas and in the spring, with the boy spending his summers in Africa. By that time, Goodall's international renown had continued to grow, thanks in part to the publication of 1971's best-seller *In the Shadow of Man*. Part memoir, part scientific exploration, the book detailed her first decade in Gombe and was hailed by the *New York Times* as "charming and relaxed."

"What is most appealing about her book is the extent to which she involves us in her 'characters,' without resorting to excessive anthropomorphism," wrote reviewer Christopher Lehmann-Haupt. "Whether these creatures are appealing because they are so human, or because humans are so apelike, is hard to say. In any case . . . it is fascinating to observe the subtle emotional interplay that preserves the community's social fabric. And it is poignant indeed to have to suffer the moments of disaster, like little Goblin's loss of his mother and his subsequent nervous deterioration, or old Mr. MacGregor's [sic] losing battle with polio."

Goodall's prose connected readers with her chimps so that their hardships felt visceral and real, yet witnessing them firsthand was even more impactful. Many of Goodall's observations during the 1970s were of a darker nature. After Flo died of natural causes in 1972, her son Flint—who had remained unusually attached to his mother, insisting on riding on her back or demanding that she groom him—fell into a depression, stopped eating, and died not long after. "Flint's death is a tragedy in every way; at the same time, it is an amazing testimony to the depth and significance of the affectionate bond which can unite a chimpanzee child to his mother," Goodall wrote in an obituary for Flo that ran in the *Times of London* on October 1, 1972.

In Bryceson, she found not only a romantic companion who shared her love of animals and fascination with the natural world, but also a powerful political ally.

Then, in 1974, Goodall watched as a violent conflict broke out among the Kasekela community that she had spent so many years observing and an offshoot group known as Kahama. "We saw adult males patrolling the boundaries of their territory, searching for sight and listening for sound of their neighbors," Goodall recalled in 2015. "If an individual 'stranger' from a neighboring community was found, he or usually she was subjected to a brutal assault and usually died of wounds sustained. Only young females, who had not yet given birth, were spared—they were actively persuaded to follow the males back into their home community."

The campaign of violence would go on for four years, as the Kasekela males killed their counterparts and three adult females and took over the territory. Beyond what was dubbed the Four Year War, Goodall's field staff separately recorded acts of cannibalism perpetrated by an adult female, Passion, and her two offspring.

"I felt I hated Passion and [her daughter] Pom at the time," Goodall said in 2015. "Unfortunately, we have seen the same behavior in other mothers over the succeeding years. These violent behaviors—boundary attacks, the Four Year War and cannibalism—forever changed my view of chimpanzees: I had thought they were so like us, but nicer. This turned out not to be true, but it is almost certain that chimpanzees cannot fully comprehend the pain and suffering they inflicted on their victims."

The early-to-mid 1970s brought further shocking travails. On the night of May 19, 1975, 40 armed men from across the border in what was then Zaire (now the Democratic Republic of Congo) burst into the research station and kidnapped four people from the camp at gunpoint, including three students from Stanford University, where Goodall had been teaching part-time as a visiting professor.

The ordeal stretched into July when the final hostage was released, but things at the research facility were never the same afterward. For Goodall to be on site, she required either government clearance or the presence of a military guard. "The kidnapping and its aftermath of bitterness and misery affected all of us who were part of it," Goodall is quoted as writing in Peterson's biography.

Even the joyous news in Goodall's life during that period would come to be tempered with sadness. In 1975, she married Derek Bryceson, a former British Royal Air Force pilot who was the only white

CONTINUED ON PAGE 62

*Goodall in the 1980s.*

CONTINUED FROM PAGE 59

member of Tanzania's parliament and was also the director of the country's National Parks. The pair had met three years earlier, when Goodall joined a group to lobby for Gombe to receive national park status. "I distinctly recall when Jane came to parliament later to show her film on the chimpanzees," Bryceson told *People* in 1977. "She made a very definite impression."

In Bryceson, she found not only a romantic companion who shared her love of animals and fascination with the natural world but also a powerful political ally. In later years, she would describe him as having been instrumental in helping her transform her scientific headquarters into the Gombe Stream National Park. "What we enjoy most is dining alone," Goodall told *People*. "The ideal life," Derek [interjected] wistfully, "would be to stay all year at Gombe, by the clear lake—far away from the city."

Although idyllic, their time together was brief. Only five years after they had married, Bryceson was diagnosed with terminal cancer, which claimed his life in a matter of months. The then 46-year-old Goodall was bereft, but she resolved to soldier on. "I just plough on and hope that, with the passing of time, I shall be able to spend more time remembering the happy days," Goodall wrote to *National Geographic*'s Mary Smith, as noted in the Peterson biography.

**THERE WAS STILL** much to be done. In 1977, the world's foremost primatologist had founded her namesake organization, the Jane Goodall Institute for Wildlife Research, Education, and Conservation, a consortium focused on continuing Goodall's chimpanzee research while also aiming to protect the chimpanzees. The animals were facing increasingly grave threats from poachers and hunters, not to mention habitat destruction owing to rapid deforestation, and Goodall vowed to use her cultural prominence to come to their aid.

It was the start of what would become the vibrant second act of Goodall's life's work, which saw her devote more of her time to outspoken activism. As she continued to appear in documentaries (including 1977's National Geographic production *Introduction to Chimpanzee Behavior*) and publish books (such as 1986's *The Chimpanzees of Gombe: Patterns of Behavior*), Goodall remained, as ever, a kind of worldwide ambassador for her beloved chimpanzees. The goodwill that greeted her wherever she went only helped her cause, allowing her to become a broader champion for animal welfare and conservation.

It was a responsibility she never took lightly.

"I feel like I've been chosen as a messenger," Goodall said in the 2020 documentary *Jane Goodall: The Hope*. "Cheers to the messengers." ☐

*Goodall began her transition out of the field in the 1980s. Here, she prepared for a presentation in Chicago in 1982; she appeared on* The Tonight Show *Starring Johnny Carson in 1984.*

# 'Being a Woman Was Crucial to My Success in a Male-Dominated Field'

In a 2018 essay for TIME, the primatologist reflected on the sexism she faced.

**BY JANE GOODALL**

**When I** was a little girl, I used to dream as a man because I wanted to do things that women didn't do back then, such as traveling to Africa, living with wild animals, and writing books. I didn't have any female explorers or scientists to look up to, but I was inspired by Dr. Dolittle, Tarzan, and Mowgli in *The Jungle Book*—all male characters. It was only my mother who supported my dream: "You'll have to work hard, take advantage of opportunities, and never give up," she'd tell me. I've shared that message with young people around the world, and so many have thanked me and said, "You taught me that because you did it, I can do it, too." I wish mum was around to hear the way her message to me has touched so many lives.

I remember a very funny time in my life just before I got to Africa. My paternal uncle was Sir Michael Spens, son of Lord Patrick Spens. Michael was keen to present me at court as a debutante—in those days, society girls had a season of dances and balls—a kind of marriage market. Obviously to me, this was completely absurd, but I had to humor Michael, and so I lined up in Buckingham Palace to shake hands with the Queen. I remember being surrounded by girls who said to me, "Don't you dream of being a lady-in-waiting?" I replied, "Absolutely not—I want to live among wild animals." They recoiled in horror. They thought I was very weird, but then I thought they were very weird, too.

I couldn't afford to go to university, so I got a secretarial job in London. Opportunity came with a letter from a school friend inviting me for a holiday to Kenya. (I worked as a waitress to save enough money to go.) And it was in Kenya that I met the eminent paleontologist Dr. Louis Leakey. He was impressed by my knowledge of African animals (I had read every book I could find) and sent me to observe chimpanzees in what was then Tanganyika. He felt that a knowledge of the primate most like us would help him to better understand the probable behavior of our Stone Age ancestors whose fossilized remains he was excavating. He took me despite my lack of academic credentials—or even because of them, as he wanted someone with a mind uncluttered by the reductionist scientific thinking of the time.

What an amazing opportunity. At first the chimpanzees ran away as soon as they saw me, but once I gained their trust, I soon realized just how similar they are to us. It was an exciting day when I observed, for the first time, a chimpanzee using and making tools to "fish" termites from their nests. At that point, National Geographic offered to continue funding my research and sent Hugo van Lawick,

*Hardly a wilting rose, Goodall spent hundreds of hours crouched in the brush in Tanzania waiting for a glimpse of the chimpanzees.*

*The press was enthralled by the idea of a woman out in the jungles of Africa, demonstrated by this headline from the* Chicago Daily Globe *in 1962 (opposite). Outside of the field, Goodall was a passionate speaker. In 1985, she addressed the National Press Club in Washington, D.C., to bring awareness to the threats facing the world's primate population.*

a talented filmmaker, to document the chimps' behaviors. A year later, Geographic wanted me to write an article for their magazine. And soon after that, they made a documentary from Hugo's film footage, narrated by Orson Welles.

I had to go to America, attend a press conference, and give a few talks. The media produced some rather sensational articles, emphasizing my blond hair and referring to my legs. Some scientists discredited my observations because of this—but that did not bother me so long as I got the funding to return to Gombe and continue my work. I had never wanted to be a scientist anyway, as women didn't have such careers in those days. I just wanted to be a naturalist. If my legs helped me get publicity for the chimps, that was useful.

After this, Louis arranged for me to go to Cambridge University, where I became the eighth person in their history to be admitted to work for a Ph.D. without a B.A. But to my dismay, I was quickly told that I had done my study all wrong. I should have numbered the chimps rather than given them names, and I could not talk about their personalities, minds, or emotions, as those features were unique to humans. I was told there is a difference between humans and all other animals. That way of thinking,

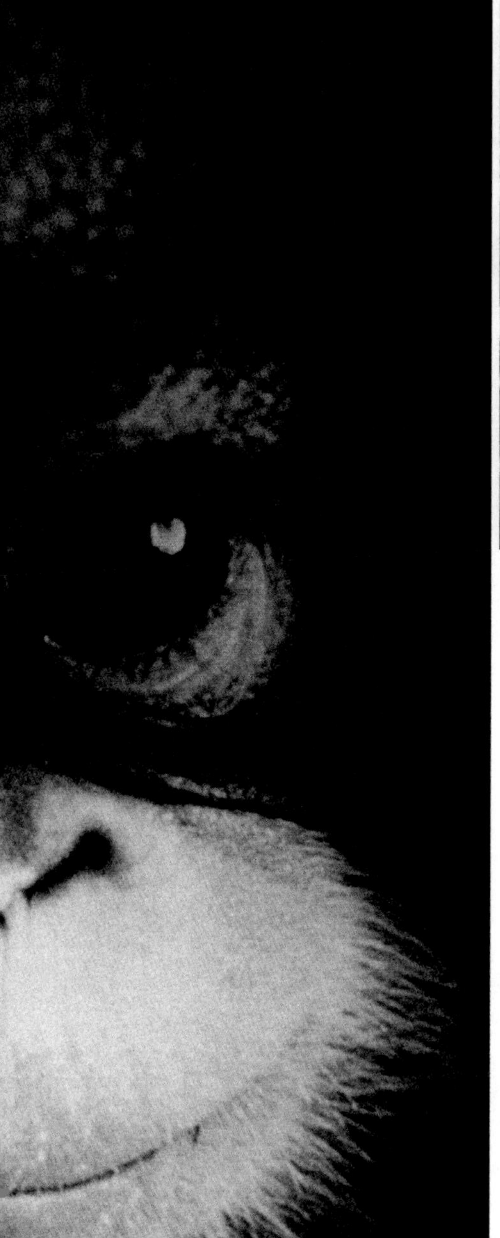

Chicago Daily

THE WORLD'S GREATEST NEWSPAPER

TUESDAY, APRIL 17, 1962

Woman Lives Alone in Jungle with Apes

of course, makes it easier to treat animals as things rather than sentient and sapient beings able to experience joy, fear, despair, and pain. Easier to work in a factory farm or medical research laboratory and for us to enjoy the sport of trophy hunting.

But I understood the true nature of animals from my childhood teacher—my dog Rusty. So I knew that in this respect the Cambridge professors were wrong, as does everyone who has shared their life in a meaningful way with a dog or a horse or a hamster or a bird. I stuck to my convictions, and because the chimpanzees are so like us biologically as well as behaviorally, gradually scientists have become less reductionist. Indeed, animal personalities and emotions are now subjects for serious study, and there is a huge amount of research being conducted on the intelligence of animals ranging from chimpanzees, elephants, and dolphins to birds, octopuses, and even some insects.

I was also told that scientists must be coldly objective and never show empathy for their "subjects." But you can make observations that are absolutely scientifically accurate even while having empathy for the being you are studying. In fact, it can sometimes provide an intuition about the meaning of a certain behavior. You can then test your intuition with scientific rigor.

In chimp society, there are good and bad mothers, and looking back over the years, we know that the offspring of mothers who were affectionate, protective but not over protective, and, above all, supportive, tend to do better and to have more self-confidence. The males tend to rise to a higher position in their hierarchy, and females are more successful as mothers, which is their main job. And throughout evolution, this was important for the human female too—they needed to be patient, quick to understand the wants and needs of their infants before they could speak, and good at keeping the peace between family members. If these qualities are, to some extent, handed down in our female genes, this may explain why women, so often, make good observers. This helped me, for Louis Leakey firmly believed that women made better field workers than men. Being a woman helped me in practical ways, too. Africa was just moving into independence and white males were still perceived as something of a threat, whereas I as a mere woman was not.

Because I succeeded in a scientific world largely dominated by men, I've been described as a feminist role model, but I never think of myself in that way. Although the feminist movement today is different, many women who have succeeded have done so by emphasizing their masculine characteristics. But we need feminine qualities to be both accepted and respected, and in many countries this is beginning to happen. I love that the new movement involves women joining their voices together on social media, thus giving a sense of solidarity.

There are indigenous people in Latin America who have a saying that their tribe is like an eagle: One wing is male and one wing is female, and only when the wings are equally strong will their tribe fly high. And this, indeed, is worth fighting for.

*Goodall, accompanied by her trusty sidekick, Mr. H, was honored at a UNESCO conference in Paris in 2024.*

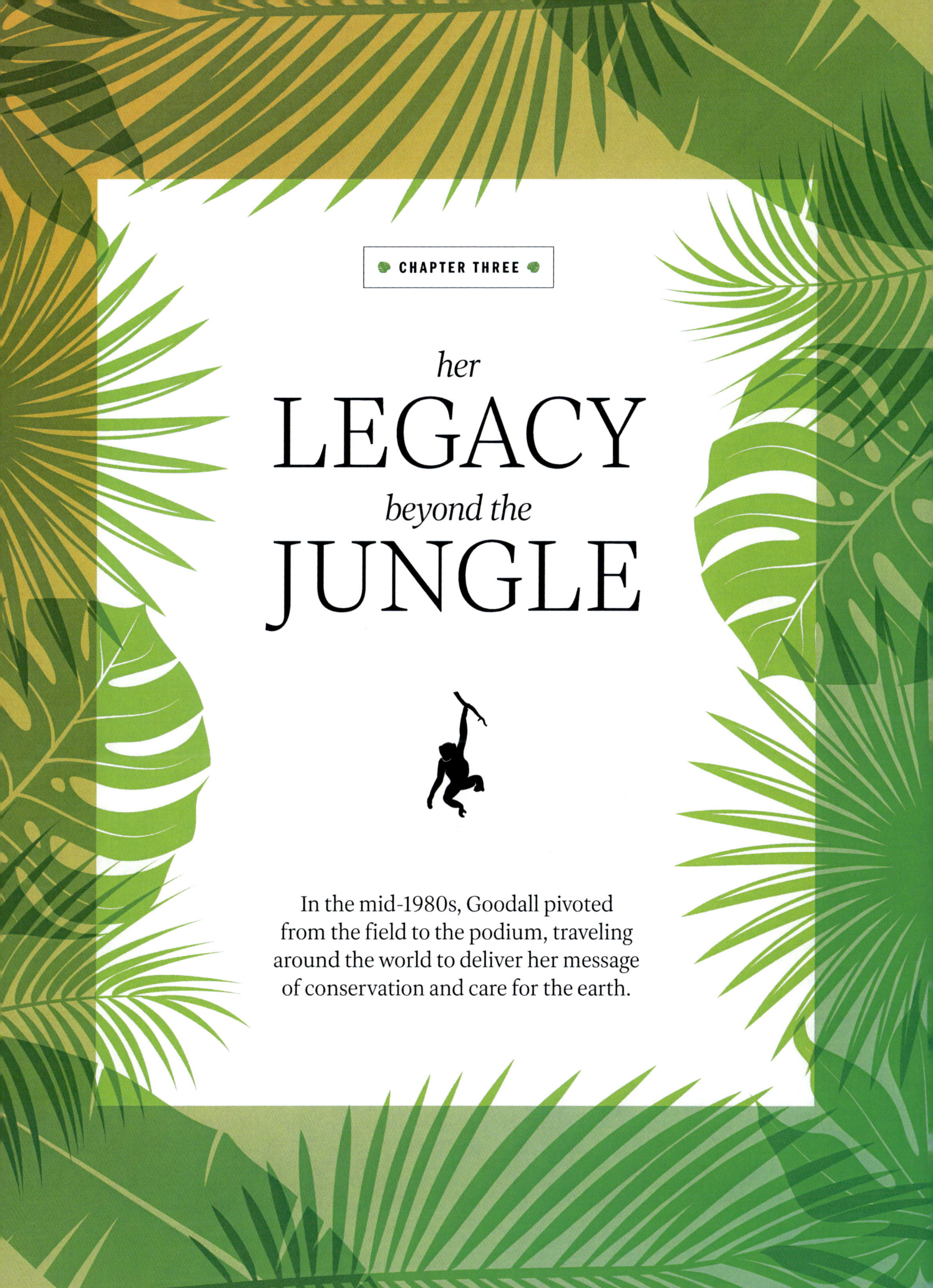

CHAPTER THREE

# *her* LEGACY *beyond the* JUNGLE

In the mid-1980s, Goodall pivoted from the field to the podium, traveling around the world to deliver her message of conservation and care for the earth.

*When Goodall visited Beijing, she was swarmed by young children asking for her autograph.*

# The Gentle Disruptor

As an environmental activist, Goodall traveled more than 300 days a year, spreading hope and reminding us that small actions make a powerful difference.

**BY LISA LOMBARDI**

IN 2003, JANE GOODALL HEARD THAT TWO young scientists without Ph.D.s were starting a study of chimpanzees in a pristine forest in the Congo that was slated for logging. Goodall had never seen another wild chimpanzee site, so she wanted to visit. She walked 12 miles through swampland and rivers that border the forest to the Goualougo Triangle—an area that was home to not only chimps but also gorillas, forest elephants, and leopards—to meet with the scientists. She was at home in the forest. "Jane was everything that we hoped she would be: insightful, humble, kind, curious, and so much fun," says Crickette Sanz, Ph.D., now chair and professor in the Department of Anthropology at Washington University in St. Louis, who was conducting the research with her now husband, David Morgan.

Sanz and Morgan were faced with a problem: The area was slated for logging. So the world-famous primatologist leapt into action. Immediately after visiting the field site, Goodall met with the president of the Republic of the Congo, Denis Sassou Nguesso, to make a case for the protection of the chimpanzees and hundreds of kilometers of pristine forest where they lived. Her lobbying efforts worked: The government extended the area of protected forests. "It would not have happened without Jane," says Sanz. "She is someone who you could always count on to follow through, whether the task was impossibly large or incredibly small."

At the time she intervened in the Congo, Goodall was almost 70 and well into her second act, working tirelessly as a conservation advocate. Up until the day she died, at the age of 91, Goodall traveled more than 300 days a year, meeting with world leaders, raising needed funds, collaborating (and chatting) with scientists, and mesmerizing everyone from schoolchildren to heads of states with her stories and mission. Through talks at local zoos and science museums, through books and documentaries, she invited ordinary people in to experience the wonderful, vulnerable world she'd seen. And she spurred them to join her in protecting our planet.

At the heart of her work, and her effectiveness, was simple storytelling, through which she opened eyes and hearts to the interconnection of humans, animals, and the planet. During this golden period of her remarkable, long life, she prioritized teaching young people and inviting them to care as much about conservation and the environment as she did. Her youth-empowerment program, Roots & Shoots, "is what she really, truly wanted to be remembered for," says anthropologist Mireya Mayor, Ph.D., Director of the Exploration and Science Communication Initiative at Florida International University in Miami, who considered Goodall a mentor and friend after meeting her at a conference in Ecuador in 2007. She inspired younger generations to "act not out of guilt but out of love for the world."

So what made Goodall transform her mission from field scientist to environmental and conservation activist? While she loved observing the chimpanzees in Gombe, Tanzania, she realized she needed to continue the work in a new way, on a new stage. This dramatic reinvention started in the 1980s, at the Lincoln Park Zoo in Chicago.

"She is someone who you could always count on to follow through, whether the task was impossibly large or incredibly small."

—CRICKETTE SANZ

**TO UNDERSTAND GOODALL'S** pivot to environmental activist, you need to travel back to 1986. Goodall was attending a Chicago conference that she helped organize: Understanding Chimpanzees. She sat in on sessions on habitat loss and animal cruelty around the world and found it "utterly shocking," she said. It opened her eyes to what she needed to do to make the biggest impact. "I arrived at the conference as a scientist," Goodall later remarked. "I left as an activist."

After that conference, Goodall changed her full-time residence from Gombe (though she would keep a presence there) to Bournemouth, in the United Kingdom. She was barely home, though. From the outset, she threw herself into traveling the globe to open eyes and fight for animal and nature conservation.

She may have had a new purpose, but it wasn't easy for Goodall to move on from her adopted homeland and beloved chimpanzees. "Leaving her long-term presence in Gombe was one of the hardest things she ever did," says Mayor. "But she did it because she knew that she could create change by getting out there and sharing the stories, much more so than if she was deep in the jungles of Africa."

Goodall felt an urgent calling to protect chimpanzees and other species, according to Richard Wrangham, the Ruth Moore Professor of Biological Anthropology, emeritus, at Harvard, and a leading researcher of chimp behavior who worked with Goodall. As he told the *Harvard Gazette* about her career pivot: "She learned more about the cruel ways in which chimps were often held in captivity, and from then on, it was conservation and care that mattered to her far more than research. I think it's part of the reason she was so successful. She was dauntingly single-minded."

As Goodall later told TIME about that moment: "After realizing what was going on, it was never quite the same, because then I felt I've got to try and save it." She had already founded the Jane Goodall Institute (JGI) in 1977 to help protect chimpanzees and their habitats and focus on environmental edu-

*Goodall at a World Wildlife Fund press conference in 1989, where it was announced that the United States had declared the African chimpanzee an endangered species.*

cation. And as she threw herself into her new work, she expanded JGI across the globe to support and fund needed conservation projects.

Right out of the gate, she became a "tireless ambassador for the planet," says Mayor. "She traveled 300 days a year until, really, her final breath. She did it not to become famous. In fact, she was in some ways an introvert, but she felt this unshakable responsibility to spread this message and awaken others."

**GOODALL WAS ESPECIALLY** interested in empowering young people to get involved in protecting nature and animals. So it was serendipitous that one day in 1991, Goodall was sitting on the porch of her house in Tanzania when a group of students came by and asked her for advice. They explained that they felt overwhelmed and discouraged by the huge issues facing the planet and wanted her help. Goodall encouraged them to get together with some friends and concentrate on small actions they could take right in their own community.

This was the birth of Roots & Shoots, Goodall's environmental and humanitarian youth-action program. Its focus, from the beginning, was to introduce kids to the importance of acting locally. Goodall's hope for Roots was "to place the power and resources for creating practical solutions to big challenges in the hands of young people." Through Roots & Shoots—which is now active in more than 70 countries—Goodall let the younger generations know they have the power to chip away at big environmental problems by making things a little better right where they live.

In Goodall's vision, everyone had the power to do something for neighbors, animals, and nature. From the beginning, Roots & Shoots drew in *all* kids—including those who might never take science after high school but loved animals or wanted to help the food insecure in their town, as well as future scientists like Serena DeStano, a junior at Northeastern University in Boston who is on the Roots & Shoots Youth Council. DeStano first got involved with Roots & Shoots as a sophomore in high school, when she planted a native garden in front of her Massachusetts home. Now studying ecology, evolutionary biology, and environmental studies, she is on to a new project: teaming up with a few friends to pilot

*In 1997, Goodall observed the chimp population from behind glass at the Taronga Zoo in Sydney, Australia. Also in Australia, Goodall listened to stories from a pair of Aboriginal dancers (opposite).*

a green roofing program in Boston to attack the climate change–related problem of the urban heat island effect.

Through her involvement with Roots & Shoots, DeStano has learned that "we all have an impact already on the world, every day that we live, in every moment," she says. "And we get to have a say in what we do and what happens to this world that we inherit, and we can try to make an impact and help make it a better place."

Through individual or group projects, kids can make the kind of impact they want. They can get involved in small, doable ways by picking a "1-click" initiative from the Roots website (for example, planting a native tree or eating meatless for one day). They can also join a challenge, such as celebrating World Chimpanzee Day in fun ways like taking a Google Street tour of Gombe. Some students, like DeStano, design their own projects with friends or mentors at school; others sign on to help with another student's project (from recycling efforts to waterway cleanups). Roots & Shoots emphasizes a 4-step process: 1) Get Engaged. 2) Observe. 3) Take Action. And 4) Celebrate.

It's Goodall's message that little acts come together in big ways that strikes a chord with DeStano. "It's really powerful because it has such a big focus on acting locally and that if we all make a difference in our own small piece of the world, that combined effort really comes together and we can make such a powerful difference together."

DeStano says that getting to meet Goodall a few times has been "the best days of my life." This college student celebrates Goodall's birthday every year by running a food drive in Boston on the big day (April 3). DeStano's favorite part is channeling Goodall and helping with environmental education programs for young students, "empowering the younger generation to feel like they can make a difference."

*Goodall at home in England. She famously told Stephen Colbert in 2024 that she prefers dogs to chimps.*
*Opposite: Goodall visited the manatees at Homosassa Springs Wildlife State Park in Florida in 2000.*

**IN THE 1990S,** Goodall deepened her commitment to fighting for the ethical treatment of animals and protecting vulnerable animals and communities around the world. In 1992, her institute opened the Tchimpounga Chimpanzee Rehabilitation Center in the Republic of Congo to care for vulnerable chimpanzees orphaned, malnourished, or injured by the illegal wildlife trade and deforestation. For more than 30 years, the sanctuary has cared for more than 200 chimpanzees.

She also focused on addressing rampant poverty in parts of Africa, which threatened the survival of the chimpanzees and other species through poaching, clearing animal habitat, and logging. In 1994, she started the Jane Goodall Institute's community-based conservation program, which invests in social programs in villages in Tanzania, Uganda, and the Democratic Republic of Congo, and enlists villagers to help with planting trees and monitoring the forest.

Through her Institute, Goodall also set up the Lake Tanganyika Catchment Reforestation and Education (TACARE) program in Western Tanzania, to, in her words, "try to improve the lives of the people in the villages around Gombe in very holistic ways." Working closely with Tanzanians who were experts in forestry and the local government, TACARE was set up to help provide people with sustainable livelihoods while also fighting the loss of natural resources in the indigenous forest.

**THOUGH GOODALL IS** best known for upending our understanding of chimpanzees and humans, she has another legacy: She helped seed our current environmental awareness. As she zigzagged the world, telling stories to everyone from first-graders to Leonardo DiCaprio (see page 91), she drew people in and welcomed them to her corner of the world. "Jane would often say that she was a storyteller first and a scientist second," Mayor says, "because she knew that the only way that you could make change is to get to people's hearts. And the only way to get to people's hearts is to tell stories, and connect them to these faraway places and animals that they may never even get the chance to see." By sharing her tales, she "planted the seed of what would become that modern environmental movement. And long before sustainability became a buzzword, she was urging everyone to see the interconnectedness of all living things," Mayor adds.

Among the many projects Goodall supported in her second act was the Gombe Ecosystem Health Project, a noninvasive long-term health-monitoring project to understand and mitigate disease outbreaks among chimpanzees. That was how Thomas Gillespie, Ph.D., a disease ecologist who is now chair of Environmental Sciences at Emory University, first met Goodall around 2004. They struck up a lifelong friendship that even turned into a partnership between Emory and Roots & Shoots.

In speaking about the problems facing the environment, Goodall had a way of communicating the big-picture stakes, Gillespie explains. "Jane helped people everywhere understand that conservation isn't just about saving animals; it's about the interconnected health of people, wildlife, and ecosystems. Long before 'One Health' or 'Planetary Health' became scientific frameworks, she was already living that truth," he says. "Jane didn't just warn us about climate change and biodiversity loss; she showed us how to respond: with curiosity, courage, and community."

Her belief in neighbors helping neighbors extended to the scientists, conservationists, and concerned citizens she got to know along the way. No matter how hectic her schedule was, Goodall usually found time to touch base with colleagues and take a moment to

*Goodall was named a U.N. Messenger of Peace by Secretary-General Kofi Annan in 2002. Opposite: Both animal advocates, Goodall and Betty White (top, in 2001) were dear friends. Goodall (bottom) at a Roots & Shoots event in 2003.*

enjoy the natural world. "My favorite memories [of Goodall] are evenings at Gombe watching the sun set over Congo on the far side of Lake Tanganyika," Gillespie says. "We'd sit barefoot on the beach, sipping whiskey, listening to the sounds of the forest shifting from day to night while the waves reached for our toes. We'd have wonderful conversations—brainstorming solutions, checking in on loved ones, or getting caught up together in our awe of nature. Her ability to stay connected to both the personal and the planetary was what made her extraordinary."

As a scientist, Gillespie was struck by another of her remarkable qualities: Although Goodall was world-famous by this point, she never stopped learning. He helped her understand the disease risks humans pose to chimpanzees and other wildlife, insights that led her to start taking precautions like keeping distance from wild chimpanzees and wearing a face mask in their presence. "She even became an advocate in our efforts to help ape tourism sites implement these precautions, which led to meaningful reductions in ape mortality," Gillespie says.

Years later, during the COVID-19 pandemic, Goodall worked hand in hand with Gillespie's team to protect Gombe's chimpanzees and the local communities, "even bringing her son and grandchildren into the effort as we constructed improved staff housing, improved community access to medical care, and modified research protocols to reduce chimpanzee exposure to potentially infected people," he says.

She didn't just preach taking action, he notes; she rolled up her sleeves and did it. "Her legacy reminds us that hope isn't naive," he says. "It requires discipline and demands persistence, empathy, and the belief that every action, no matter how small, matters."

**DURING HER ACTIVIST** years, no matter how urgent or busy the fundraising and speaking mission got, Goodall never lost touch with what Mayor calls "human Jane." She supported and worked with her global community of scientists. She kept in touch with many, like Sanz, who she had visited in the Congo all those years ago. "On that same day that she might be meeting with a world leader or addressing an international assembly," Sanz notes, "she would send you a handwritten note to remind you of some small shared moments and thank you for the time together. Jane was one of the most truly genuine people to have ever graced this planet. She had a way of connecting with people that did not require any fanfare."

In city after city, she made time to break bread (or share a tumbler of whiskey) with other environmental stewards. "After she visited us in Congo," Sanz adds, "Jane was wonderful about keeping in touch and letting us know when we would be in the same part of the world. We would get a personal email that she would be in Entebbe at a conference we were attending, a phone message that she was available for a stroll in Kyoto, a text that she was arriving in St. Louis soon, or that she had an evening free in Chicago. I marvel at how she managed to fit quality time with us into her busy schedule."

She also shared notes. One core mission of the Jane Goodall Institute is to solve the planet's biggest conservation challenges. Goodall knew that started with collaborative science, some of it building upon the work she had done in the fields decades earlier. The institute maintained long-term research projects in Gombe and other places in Africa. JGI also funded other scientists' research on habitat loss. Most important, Goodall's organization shared its data assets with scientists around the world, to encourage interdisciplinary research and accelerate solutions that would help the planet.

**DESCRIBED BY THOSE** who knew her as humble and even introverted, Goodall "never sought the spotlight," says Mayor. But her environmental advocacy thrust her onto a world stage. She earned support for her pet projects from billionaires like Jeff Bezos, whose Bezos Earth Fund donated $5 million in 2024 toward her work on biodiversity loss in the Democratic Republic of Congo and the Republic of Congo.

Her dedication to conservation and humanitarian action earned her accolades around the globe. In 2002, United Nations Secretary-General Kofi Annan appointed Goodall a U.N. Messenger of Peace, the highest honor of the United Nations for global citizens, for her work to create a more peaceful world through Roots & Shoots. Two years later, she was made a Dame Commander of the Order of the British Empire (DBE) by Queen Elizabeth II for "services to the environment and animal welfare." In 2006, Goodall received a French Legion of Honor, the country's most prestigious award. And in

CONTINUED ON PAGE 82

# The Touching Story Behind Why Jane Carried a Stuffed Monkey Everywhere for Decades

Mr. H, a plush and beloved companion, traveled to more than 60 countries with Goodall.

**BY KELLI BENDER**

**One of** Jane Goodall's final public appearances was at the 2025 Forbes Sustainability Leaders Summit on September 22, where she was joined by her constant companion, Mr. H, a worn stuffed monkey that had been with Goodall on almost every interview and public outing since the pair first met in 1996. She and the toy she described as her "mascot" traveled to more than 60 countries together, spreading awareness about the importance of protecting the planet and all of its inhabitants.

According to the Jane Goodall Institute, Mr. H arrived in Goodall's life as a birthday gift given to her by a friend named Gary Haun.

The plush is named, in fact, to honor Haun, a U.S. Marine who "lost his eyesight in a helicopter crash" at the age of 21 and decided to try being a magician, despite many people telling him that his vision loss would make the goal impossible.

Haun "went on to become a successful magician," according to the institute, as well as to climb Mt. Kilimanjaro and skydive, all while being blind.

It was because of this perseverance that Goodall kept Haun's gift by her side.

"[Haun's] so good that he does shows for kids and will say at the end, 'Hey, guess what—I'm blind,' because they never know," Goodall shared in a 2024 Instagram video for her institute, adding that Haun had inspired her to adopt Mr. H as a mascot to remind her that nothing is impossible.

In that same social media post, Goodall noted that some people think she carries Mr. H because he's a chimpanzee.

But she explained that the plush toy isn't a stuffed chimpanzee at all.

"Gary initially thought he was giving her a chimpanzee plushie, until she had him feel that Mr. H had a tail (chimpanzees and other great apes don't have tails, but monkeys do)," the Jane Goodall Institute added in the post.

Although there is only one Mr. H, Goodall's fans can get a Mr. H Junior for themselves from the Jane Goodall Institute, which offers the plushies so others can "spread Jane's message of hope and peace wherever you go."

*Mr. H—who has made acquaintances with a host of bold names, including actor Harrison Ford and former Canadian Prime Minister Justin Trudeau—posed for a portrait with Goodall in Paris in 2024.*

CONTINUED FROM PAGE 79

January 2025, President Joe Biden awarded Goodall the Presidential Medal of Freedom, the highest civilian honor in the United States.

Over the course of her career, she wrote more than 30 books for adults and children, half of which were written during her final decades. It's no accident that five penned during this period have the word "hope" in the title, including 2021's *The Book of Hope: A Survival Guide for Trying Times*, which has been translated into more than 20 languages.

All the while, Goodall was filling auditoriums at schools from University of Southern California to Duke University to the University of Cambridge. To a generation that grew up during a global pandemic and a time of rapidly accelerating climate crisis, Goodall's dogged optimism and emphasis on pooled effort struck a chord. "Especially in times like these, it can be very easy to feel a little hopeless and discouraged," Northeastern student DeStano says. "One of my favorite messages from Dr. Goodall is that hope is not a passive feeling, but it's an action and something we have to choose every day. "

Goodall understood that when we do one small thing to alleviate an issue facing animals or neighbors close to home, we feel motivated to keep on helping. "Doing something like planting a native garden or running a food drive and seeing the direct benefits and impacts that your work has, no matter what scale it is, is really inspiring," DeStano says, "because you can be like, 'Whoa, I did this. I helped in some way.' "

But to inspire the younger generations to care en masse, you need to engage them and meet them where they are. Goodall understood this well, and she continued to find new ways to connect. In 2019, JGI partnered with National Geographic to open *Becoming Jane*, an interactive traveling exhibit focused on Goodall's field work. Through dozens of documentaries and films, including the children's series *Jane* on Apple TV, generations of young fans got to meet, and fall in love with, the animals and planet she loved. She even launched a podcast, aptly titled *Hopecast*, which featured contemporary thought leaders like the comedy writer and director Adam McKay.

Maybe the most surprising place Goodall popped up, though, was on a TV show called *Expedition Bigfoot*. This unexpected 2022 appearance came about because Mayor was cast on the show in the role of scientific expert. When she was first approached about it, Mayor worried about her legacy and what her peers might say, so she reached out to her mentor and "north star," Goodall, to ask, "What should

*Goodall filmed the documentary* Jane's Journey *in 2010. The primatologist "went ape" with a chimpanzee in 2009 (opposite).*

I do?" Goodall's reply? "Who cares what anyone else thinks?" (Though she said it in raunchier language.) "Then she shared stories that locals in Ecuador and other parts of the world had shared with her about Bigfoot," Mayor recounts. "And she said, 'I actually think it's very possible. And I think exploration is always worthwhile and curiosity is at the heart of science.' So she encouraged me to do it." Goodall started sending Mayor dozens of emails about Bigfoot "at all hours of the night, because Jane worked until late into the night." So on a whim, Mayor invited her mentor to join her on the episode to discuss Bigfoot on camera, and to her surprise, the world's most famous primatologist said yes.

The unexpected guest spot is a window into how Goodall approached teaching science. She knew that to get people engaged in science, you "have to find that thing that sparked someone's curiosity," Mayor says. "She knew that she could speak to that, and connect to that, and then they were engaged and they were hooked and they cared. And that's what she ultimately wanted, is for people to care."

**EVEN AS GOODALL** hit her eighties, she kept traveling and fighting to protect vulnerable regions of the world. In 2023, she had a big win: The Jane Goodall Institute launched the Hope In Action project in Western Tanzania, with support from the U.S. Agency for International Development (USAID), to expand sustainable development and habitat restoration in the area. But in 2025, the Trump administration dismantled USAID, which meant the project lost almost $30 million in funding.

Despite the setback, Goodall was determined to hang onto her can-do attitude, Wrangham told the *Harvard Gazette*: "She absolutely felt that it was important for her to be an optimist because people need hope. People need to be motivated to do good

*Goodall at home among the chimps while filming* Jane's Journey.

things: good for themselves, good for the planet, good for their communities, good for nature . . . What did she really think? There's no question the difficulties got to her, but at the same time, I think that she genuinely felt that there are reasons for hope. One of the most important sources of hope for her was the indomitable human spirit. If you can remind people that if you try hard enough you can do anything—her mother's message—then good things will happen."

That is what Mayor most admired too: "her unwavering hope. Even in the face of overwhelming loss—disappearing forests, endangered species, and growing apathy—she never lost faith in humans' ability to do better."

A year before her death, Goodall gave an hour-long talk at Florida International University, then sat on stage with Mayor for another hour fielding the students' questions. "She was 90 and she held this audience of 3,000 people spellbound. Nobody moved out of their seats, nobody checked their phones," Mayor says. After the lecture, Goodall took Mayor back to her hotel and broke out the scotch. "After we toasted, that's when human Jane came alive," Mayor says. "Her guard down, her stories were flowing, and she'd go from stories of her beloved chimps and then start talking about these unforgettable encounters with people like Mikhail Gorbachev. And maybe my favorite story was when she met Michael Jackson after he'd asked her to come to Neverland Ranch. His chimp Bubbles was having behavioral issues, and he thought maybe Bubbles was depressed. One of the things that we laughed about was when she said, 'I had just met Michael and he brought me back to his bedroom and we laid in his bed and watched chimp movies and talked about Bubbles,'" Mayor says. "Her stories were always this mix of profound and funny and completely unfiltered."

> "One of the most important sources of hope for [Jane] was the indomitable human spirit."
>
> —RICHARD WRANGHAM

She brought that down-to-earth warmth on stage, night after night. Decades after Goodall visited Sanz in the Goualougo Triangle, the pair reunited in 2022, when the almost 90-year-old primatologist spoke at WashU. "I remember preparing an elaborate script, which Jane made fun of. It was then cast aside and we just talked as friends," Sanz says. "The crowd was captivated by her."

Goodall never lost her ability to spark a crowd's curiosity or wonder. "Jane gave the movement its soul and she made environmentalism deeply personal," Mayor adds, "which I think is very different than had ever been done before."

Throughout her remarkable second act as a conservationist, Emory's Gillespie says, she retained a quality that is often in short supply: "She was a radical listener; even after decades of global fame, she listened more than she spoke. She never lectured people into caring; she invited them," he says. "That invitation changed the world."

In September 2025, Goodall spent the final weeks of her life doing what she loved: fighting for the planet and its inhabitants. Just days before her death, she reached out to Spanish-American restaurateur José Andrés, who founded the global food-relief charity World Central Kitchen, to see what she could do to alleviate the suffering in Gaza and Ukraine.

Her message, until the very end, revolved around hope. "She believed hope is not passive; it's a choice we make every day through our actions," Mayor says. "She believed that every single person could make a difference. That was her rare magic. She made everyone, from a child to a head of state, feel seen and valued, and, most important, capable of changing the world." ◻

*Goodall received a standing ovation at the World Forum in the Hague in 2023. Her son, "Grub," all grown up in 2018 (above, left).*

# Jane in Pop Culture

A vibrant voice and game guest, Goodall left her mark on the zeitgeist.

**BY EMMA MURPHY**

**Jane Goodall** was a voice actor, social media influencer, and frequenter on talk shows—Jimmy Fallon even had a portrait of Goodall in his home. Her classy, soft-spoken ways and her love for dogs made the primatologist beloved outside of the scientific community, and Goodall used her notability to draw awareness to her conservation efforts. At 91 years old, Goodall filmed TikToks and accumulated almost 2 million followers on Instagram, reaching a new audience and cementing herself in 21st-century pop culture. Here are her noteworthy cultural moments.

## Far Side Comics

*1987*

What at first appeared to be a brief spat between Goodall and Far Side writer Gary Larson turned into a memorable moment that underscored the scientist's lighthearted sense of humor. In a 1987 strip, two chimps sit in a tree; the female chimp picks a hair off the male's shoulder as she says, "Well, well—another blond hair... Conducting a little more 'research' with that Jane Goodall tramp?" Shortly after the comic's release, the editor of the *Arizona Daily Star* received a letter from the executive director of the Jane Goodall Institute stating, "The cartoon was incredibly offensive and in such poor taste that readers might well question the editorial judgment of running such an atrocity in a newspaper that reputes to be supplying the news to persons with a better than average intelligence. The cartoon and its message were absolutely stupid." But as it turned out, Goodall hadn't even seen the strip at the time the letter was written; when she did, she thought it was so funny that she licensed the image for T-shirts and sold them through the Institute.

## *The Wild Thornberrys*

*2001*

Goodall premiered her voice acting career in the episode titled "The Trouble With Darwin," which celebrates the opening of a chimpanzee sanctuary. The show's main character, Eliza, who can talk to animals, tells Goodall (who plays herself) that she named a goldfish after her. Though Goodall is certainly no professional actor, her British accent and excellent impressions of chimps made her small cameo in the Nickelodeon show memorable for many fans.

## *The Simpsons*

*2019*

Goodall once again played herself, this time in the thirty-first season of *The Simpsons*, but her affinity for the show stretches back to the series' second-ever episode, in which Bart Simpson's principal suggests that he watch his fellow fourth-graders in the same way that Jane Goodall observes chimps. After seeing the episode, Goodall sent a fan letter to the show's creators, as well as an autographed copy of her book. But that didn't stop the show's writers from satirizing her. In a season 12

*Goodall appeared on a host of TV series, including the AppleTV+ show* Jane *(above) with Mason Blomberg and Ava Louise Murchison. She also lent her voice to* The Wild Thornberrys *and* The Simpsons *(opposite).*

episode titled "Simpson Safari," the family ventures to Tanzania, where they discover a corrupt woman scientist enslaving chimpanzees to mine for diamonds. Goodall didn't hold a grudge, and almost 20 years later, she appeared in the episode "Gorillas on the Mast." This time, the writers glorified Goodall, with daughter Lisa calling the primatologist her "hero."

## Barbie

*2022*

A partnership between Mattel and the Jane Goodall Institute turned the Brit into a Barbie, and in classic fashion, the young blonde sports long plastic legs, a sleek ponytail, and a matching safari outfit (chimp sidekick included). But this traditional doll comes with a twist—it's made from recycled ocean-bound plastic and is certified carbon neutral. Goodall said she hoped the collection would inspire young people to join her in conservation work and "remind them they can be anything, anywhere—on the field, in the lab, and at the table." The doll originally sold for $35 but is now a collector's item, often listed for five times its ticket price on the resale market.

## Lego

*2022*

For a two-week period in March 2022, Lego fans had the opportunity to receive a 276-piece Jane Goodall gift set, with purchase, to mark International Women's Day. This extremely limited-edition toy features a jungle scene with chimpanzees in the

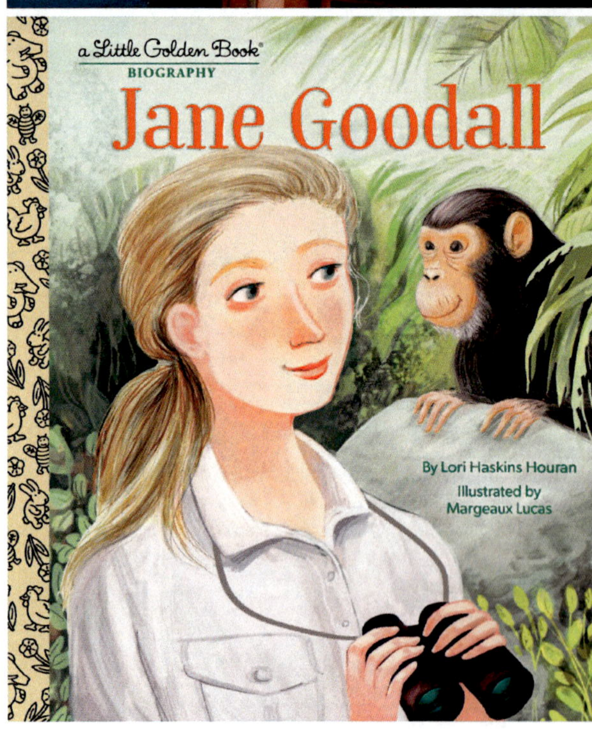


*Clockwise from top: Goodall toasted with Colbert in 2024; was given the Barbie treatment in 2022; and is the subject of a Little Golden Book.*

trees and on the forest floor along with a gray-haired Goodall standing by a Tanzanian river. For sustainability purposes, the set is made in part from eco-friendly plastic sourced from sugar cane.

### *Jane* (Apple TV+ Series)

*2023*

Based on Goodall's work, the series follows 9-year-old Jane Garcia (accompanied by her chimp friend Greybeard), who tries to save a new endangered animal or tackle an emerging environmental issue in each of the series's 20 episodes. The show is entertaining for antsy children viewers, and it's also educational: Each episode features an interview with a real-life scientist who can speak to the complicated matters highlighted in the show.

### *Jane Goodall: A Little Golden Book Biography*

*2024*

A cartoon Goodall made her way onto the front cover of the classic golden-spined children's tome. The 24-page picture book tells the story of Goodall's life in adorable illustrations that bring young tots to the lush green jungles of Africa. It's just one of many kids' books she appeared in over the years. Jane Goodall book club, anyone?

### *The Late Show With Stephen Colbert*

*2024*

One of Goodall's last—and perhaps most memorable—late-night appearances was on Colbert's couch, where the two kicked off their conversation over a glass of bourbon. She casually noted that chimps will drink liquor if they're given a taste and said they sometimes drink fermented palm liquid from the trees. Over the years, Goodall was also a frequent guest on *The Tonight Show With Jimmy Fallon.* After Goodall's death, the show's YouTube channel released a commemorative video. Though often described as an introvert, Goodall was game to spread her message about conservation in TV interviews like these, and always did so with a soft laugh and a smile.

# Honoring Her Life's Work

## Goodall was named to the TIME 100 in 2018, with actor Leonardo DiCaprio penning a moving tribute.

**BY LEONARDO DiCAPRIO**

**I admired** Jane Goodall long before we ever met. I knew of her landmark work with chimpanzees in Gombe. I had read about her, read books written by her, but it was only when I got to spend more time with Jane a few years ago that I truly felt I was in the presence of one of the most impactful and important leaders on the planet. She chose to go to Tanzania at the age of 26 to study chimpanzees, and the research she conducted there, in the jungle at the eastern shore of Lake Tanganyika, ended up changing behavioral science forever.

Since then she has committed her life to environmental protection. Even now, at the young age of 85, Jane spends nearly every day spreading optimism and raising awareness worldwide; hers is a powerful message to protect the inherent rights of every living creature, to provide hope for future generations, and to sound an urgent call against the greatest environmental threat of all—climate change. Anyone who has heard her speak, or heard her story, has been mesmerized by her life's work and moved by her philanthropic legacy.

She has become a very close friend—and it is this friendship and unwavering commitment to our shared causes for which I, and so many others worldwide, am forever grateful.

*DiCaprio is an Oscar-winning actor, a producer, and an environmental advocate.*

# A Final Plea for Trees

A frequent TIME contributor, Goodall wrote her last piece for the publication in 2021, advocating for forest protection and restoration.

**BY JANE GOODALL**

**Viewed from** outer space, Earth is a remarkable, vibrant planet—blue waters, majestic mountains, vast areas of green forests. It's an inspiring, stunning display of all the perfect elements to support the billions of diverse life-forms who call this planet home.

But the view from the surface offers a starkly different story. Colonialism and the industrial revolution created a global extraction economy with little regard for the natural systems that sustain all life.

And one of the most tragic consequences of this extractive economy is the staggering loss of half of the planet's trees. Where once our planet was home to 6 trillion trees, only 3 trillion remain. And half of that loss has occurred in only the past 100 years—barely a blink of an eye considering the millions of years it took to create Earth's biodiverse landscapes.

Our planet has sustained an unspeakable loss, yet forests continue to be deliberately destroyed at the rate of about an acre and a half a second, as they are permanently leveled to create inexpensive land used for large-scale beef, palm oil, soy, and paper production. Short-term profit continues to be prioritized over the near- and long-term health of our planet. If this madness continues at the current rate, by the end of this century, the modest green landscape that can be seen today from outer space will be a thing of the past.

Every forest that is burned and bulldozed releases massive amounts of stored carbon into the atmosphere. When a forest is lost, especially a dense tropical forest, so too is its potential to absorb carbon pollution.

This willful destruction of forests is so much more consequential than most people realize. Trees, forests, and all plant life have a crucial role in balancing and maintaining the cycles of life on our planet. They provide food, water, shelter, and medical cures. They create the oxygen we breathe and absorb the carbon dioxide that threatens our climate. Deforestation and other land-use disruptions account for a staggering 23 percent of the world's greenhouse gas emissions.

To make matters worse, severe drought and record high temperatures have dramatically increased the severity of wildfires and lengthened wildfire seasons around the world. The recent Siberian wildfires (which have received disgracefully little media coverage) are larger than all of the planet's fires combined. They are so out of control that governments have given up on trying to put them out.

Between record-setting forest loss and recent warnings about the rapidly ticking climate clock, protecting and restoring our forests must become one of the highest of our planetary priorities. In fact, natural climate solutions, including the restoration and management of forests, grasslands and wetlands, can deliver up to one-third of the emission reductions needed by 2030.

Although many good people,

*Goodall visited the CosmoCaixa Museum of Science in Barcelona, Spain, which features a small reproduction of the Amazon Rainforest, in 2018.*

*As part of her Roots & Shoots program, Goodall helped plant 10 crab apple trees in Boulder, Colorado.*

organizations, and governments are fighting against the economic forces driving the destruction of our planet, it simply is not enough. This is why the United Nations recently launched its Decade of Ecosystem Restoration and supports the Trillion Tree Campaign, a global call to arms to save and restore our forests. And why we have launched our grassroots initiative, Trees for Jane, to do our part to support this ambitious challenge. We want to inspire everyone worldwide to combat our climate crisis by adding new funding and momentum to ongoing efforts to stop deforestation and restore lost forests. We also want to encourage people to plant and nurture their own trees to help our cause and better value the fragility of nature.

Planting trees and protecting and restoring forests are not new solutions—they are tried and tested. What is new is the latest IPCC report that paints a more dire picture of the climate emergency than ever before. Our response must be to act now—at unprecedented levels!

One trillion trees planted and protected is a big number, even over a 10-year period. But if everyone pitches in, we have a fighting chance to make a difference. Let's help give everyone a way to join a global movement to save forests and restore biodiverse landscapes. Let's help reverse the worst impacts of climate change. Together, let's create a sustainable planet for generations to come. Join us today. Let's give our planet a new reason for hope.

# TIME

**Editor in Chief** Sam Jacobs
**Managing Editor** Lily Rothman
**Creative Director** D.W. Pine


# Jane Goodall
## 1934–2025


**People Inc. PREMIUM PUBLISHING**
**Vice President, Editor in Chief** Kostya Kennedy
**Creative Director** Gary Stewart
**Photo Director** C. Tiffany Lee
**Editorial Operations Director** Jamie Roth Major
**Editor** Amy Wilkinson
**Senior Art Director** Lan Yin Bachelis
**Photo Editor** Robert Conway
**Writers** Kelli Bender, Sharon Cotliar, Ava Erickson, Jeffrey Kluger, Daniel S. Levy, Lisa Lombardi, Gina McIntyre, Emma Murphy, Rich Sands
**Manager, Editorial Operations** Gina Scauzillo
**Associate Manager, Editorial Operations** Ariel Davis
**Copy Chief** Tracy Guth Spangler
**Copy Editor** Diane M. Pavia
**Reporter** Tresa McBee
**Photo Assistant** Nicoleta Papavasilakis
**Production Designer** Sandra Jurevics
**Premedia Trafficking Supervisor** Jacqueline Beard
**Director, Premedia Imaging** Michael Sturtz
**Premedia Color Quality Analyst** John Santucci
**Production Director** Patrick McGowan
**Production Managers** Ashley Schaubroeck, Trevi Jones, April Gross
**Senior Quality Director** Joe Kohler

**Vice President & General Manager** Jeremy Biloon
**Executive Publishing Director** Megan Pearlman
**Senior Director, Brand Marketing** Jean Kennedy
**Associate Director, Brand Marketing** Katherine Barnet
**Associate Director, Business Development and Partnerships** Nina Reed
**Brand Manager, Brand Marketing** Mia Rinaldi
**Associate Brand Manager, Brand Marketing** Gabby Amello

**Special thanks** Brad Beatson, Cheryl Silver

**People Inc.**
**Chief Business Officer, President Lifestyle** Alysa Borsa

People Inc. MPA THE ASSOCIATION OF MAGAZINE MEDIA

*A young Goodall appeared with a chimp on a Sierra Leone postage stamp.*

# Credits


**Front cover**
MTI, Barnabas Honeczy/AP (inset) Hugo van Lawick/ The Jane Goodall Institute

**Back cover**
(from top) Hugo van Lawick/The Jane Goodall Institute; Danita Delimont/ Alamy

**1** CBS/Getty Images **2-3** Penelope Breese/Liaison/ Getty Images **4** Vincent Calmel **6** CBS/Getty Images **7** Bobby Yip/Reuters/ Redux

**A Life in Photos**
**8-9** Hugo van Lawick/ The Jane Goodall Institute **10-11** (from left) AP; Bettmann/Getty Images **12-13** Hugo van Lawick/ The Jane Goodall Institute **14-15** The Jane Goodall Institute **16-17** Prichard/ EPA/Shutterstock **18-19** from left) Robert Ratzer/ The Jane Goodall Institute; Benedikt von Loebell/ World Economic Forum **20-21** Jeff Spicer/Getty Images **22-23** Manuel Balce Ceneta/AP

**Chapter 1: The Early Years**
**25** The Jane Goodall Institute/Courtesy of the Goodall Family **26** The Jane Goodall Institute/ Courtesy of the Goodall Family **28** (right) AF Fotografie/Alamy **29** The Jane Goodall Institute/Courtesy of the Goodall Family **30** Bettmann/Getty Images **32-33** (from left) The Jane Goodall Institute; Universal Images Group/Alamy; Album/Zuma

**Chapter 2: Her Life Among the Chimps**
**35** CBS/Getty Images **36** Hugo van Lawick/The Jane Goodall Institute **38-39** Smith Archive/Alamy (2) **40-41** Hugo van Lawick/ The Jane Goodall Institute; Smith Archive/Alamy **42-43** (from left) Edwin Sampson/Daily Mail/ Shutterstock; Keystone/ Hulton Archive/Getty Images **44-45** Hugo van Lawick/ The Jane Goodall Institute **46-47** (clockwise from left) Hugo van Lawick/ The Jane Goodall Institute; Abramorama/Everett Collection (3) **48-49** Everett Collection **50-51** Disney General Entertainment Content/Getty Images (2) **52-53** Fotos International/ Getty Images **54-55** Fotos International/Getty Images **56-57** (from left) Hulton Archive/Getty Images; American Broadcasting Companies/Getty Images **58** The Jane Goodall Institute **60-61** ITV/ Shutterstock **62-63** (from left) Ron Tom/NBC/NBCU Photo Bank/Getty Images; Charles Knoblock/AP **64-65** Hugo van Lawick/ The Jane Goodall Institute **66-67** (from left) Bettmann/ Getty Images; Abramorama/Everett Collection

**Chapter 3: Her Legacy Beyond the Jungle**
**68** Mary-Lou Mauricio/ Hans Lucas/Redux **70-71** Natalie Behring/Reuters/ Redux **73** Renato Rotolo/ AFP/Getty Images **74-75** Megan Lewis/Reuters/ Redux (2) **76-77** Jillian Edelstein/Camera Press/ Redux; St Petersburg Times/ZUMA/Alamy **78-79** (clockwise from left) Henny Ray Abrams/AFP/Getty Images; Nick Ut/AP; David S. Holloway/Getty Images **80-81** Joel Saget/AFP/ Getty Images **82-83** (from left) Europa Press/Abaca/ Sipa USA/AP; Animal Planet/Everett Collection **84-85** Animal Planet/ Everett Collection **86-87** (from left) Jeff Spicer/ Getty Images; Ramon van Flymen/ANP/AFP/Getty Images **88** (bottom) Fox/ Everett Collection **89** Apple TV+/Everett Collection **90-91** (clockwise from top left) Scott Kowalchyk/ CBS/Getty Images; Mark Sullivan/Alamy Live News; Mattel **92-93** Enric Fontcuberta/EPA-EFE/ Shutterstock **94-95** (from left) David Jennings/Digital First Media/Boulder Daily Camera/Getty Images; Peregrine/Alamy

**96** Daniela Matejschek

"I want you to understand that we are part of the natural world. And even today, when the planet is dark, there still is hope. Don't lose hope."

—JANE GOODALL ON NETFLIX'S *FAMOUS LAST WORDS*

Made in United States
North Haven, CT
09 January 2026